SEASONED

Over 100 Recipes That Maximize Flavor Inside and Out

13-Digit ISBN: 978-1-60433-963-5
10-Digit ISBN: 1-60433-963-2

This book may be ordered by mail from the publisher. Please include $5.99 for postage and handling. Please support your local bookseller first!

Books published by Cider Mill Press Book Publishers are available at special discounts for bulk purchases in the United States by corporations, institutions, and other organizations. For more information, please contact the publisher.

Cider Mill Press Book Publishers
"Where Good Books Are Ready for Press"
PO Box 454
12 Spring Street
Kennebunkport, Maine 04046
Visit us online!
www.cidermillpress.com

Typography: Black Jack, Garamond, Gotham
Image Credits: Images on pages 13, 17, 18, 22, 25, 30, 33, 37, 39, 41, 46, 59, 60, 63, 67, 76, 84, 97, 98, 101, 103, 105, 109, 110, 123, 126, 135, 137, 142, 149, 161, 171, 175, 183, 185, 189, 193, 194, 197, 198, 201, 202, 205, 206, 209, 210, 213, 215, 217, 218, 221, 222, 225, and 226 courtesy of Cider Mill Press Book Publishers LLC.
Front cover image © StockFood / People Pictures
All other images used under official license from Shutterstock.com.
Cover image: Rib Eye with Salsa Verde & Porcini Mushroom Salt, see page 86
Back cover image: Leg of Lamb with Rosemary & Mustard Marinade, see page 128

Printed in China

1 2 3 4 5 6 7 8 9 0

First Edition

SEASONED

SEASONED

Over 100 Recipes That
Maximize Flavor Inside and Out

CIDER MILL PRESS

BOOK PUBLISHERS
KENNEBUNKPORT, MAINE

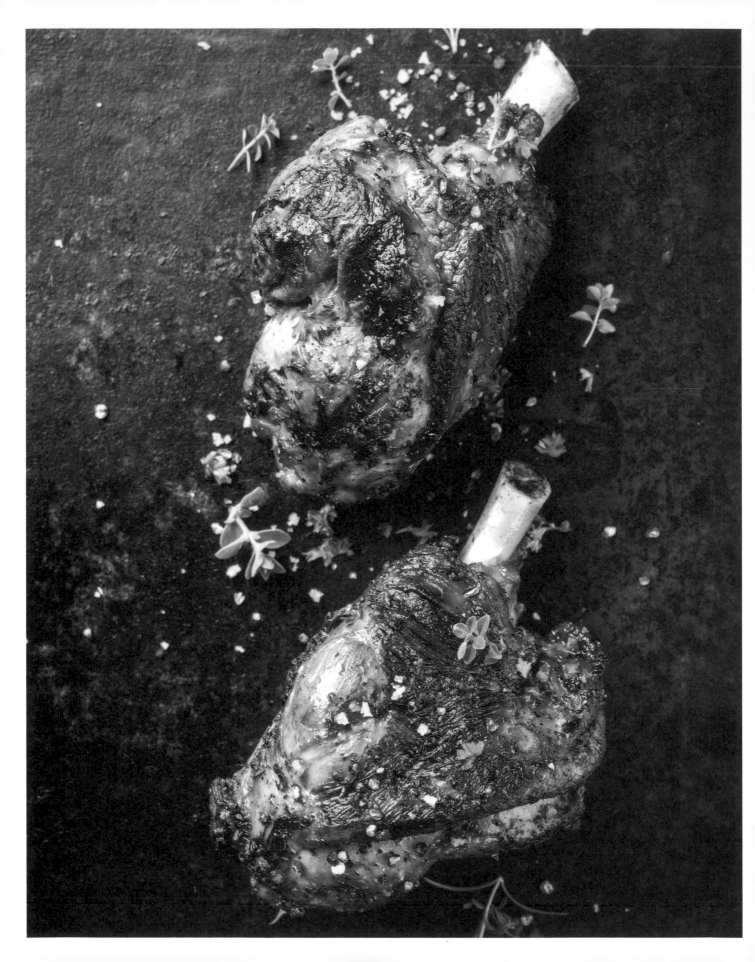

TABLE *of* CONTENTS

❋ ❋ ❋

INTRODUCTION · 7

Chapter 1: POULTRY · 11

Chapter 2: BEEF · 57

Chapter 3: PORK · 91

Chapter 4: LAMB · 115

Chapter 5: SEAFOOD · 139

Chapter 6: VEGETABLES · 179

Index · 233

INTRODUCTION

❋ ❋ ❋

Seasonings make up the line that separates great cooks from mediocre ones, and memorable food from standard fare. Human history is littered with testaments to this fact: wars have been fought over access to the most unique spices on the planet, and every culture has used them to define both their culinary palate and sense of identity.

For some, the connotations of the word "spice" cause them to turn away, preferring the safe space blander ingredients provide. But those who appreciate good food understand the miracles that can be wrought when the right spices are utilized to enhance how food tastes. Seasoning is not limited to the spicy, the peppery, the savory, but instead embraces all aspects of flavor, from the illusive umami to the sweet embrace of honey and the refreshing tartness of citrus. And sometimes, it is simply a matter of salting properly.

In order to truly embrace the wonders of a well-seasoned dish, you need to be willing to add one ingredient: time. A good marinade can take hours to develop, and some spices require cooking times that would make a kitchen novice balk. But once you cut into a short rib with a buttery texture, or experience the dynamic play of flavors the marinade lends the humble flank steak in carne asada, you will understand the immense potential time and patience unlock in the kitchen.

Experimenting with bold seasonings carries more than just the expectation of great flavors, it opens a whole new side of cooking, orients one's mind in an entirely new direction. Foods you never knew you could love will become dinner staples with the right seasoning, and family favorites can be reinvigorated with a simple dash of something new. So open your mind and step outside your comfort zone, 'tis the season to revolutionize your kitchen practice.

CHAPTER 1

POULTRY

It could be argued that chicken, turkey, and other poultry are the ideal comfort foods. Accessible, affordable, nutritious, and appealing to the eye, they make their way into our family gatherings, take up the center of a whole holiday, and slide effortlessly into the gap between party food and a full meal.

What makes these birds so versatile? Their ability to absorb whatever flavor they are cooked in. Whether glazing a batch of wings, or simply adding a touch of spice to a turkey breast, poultry is one of the best vehicles for bold flavor experiments, as there's little worry of overpowering the meat. Once you sink your teeth into Coconut Curry Chicken with Basmati Rice (see page 20) or the Chipotle Chicken Enchiladas (see pages 16–17), you'll understand that these birds can sing any tune you put in front of them.

Chicken & Sausage Cacciatore with Rice

YIELD: **6 SERVINGS**

ACTIVE TIME: **25 MINUTES**

TOTAL TIME: **6 HOURS AND 15 MINUTES**

Tender chicken thighs, sweet Italian sausage, oregano, and a scoop of salty Parmesan cheese combine to create a mouthwatering main course.

INGREDIENTS

1 LB. SWEET ITALIAN SAUSAGE

6 BONELESS, SKINLESS CHICKEN THIGHS

1 (28 OZ.) CAN OF WHOLE SAN MARZANO TOMATOES

1 (28 OZ.) CAN OF DICED TOMATOES

⅔ CUP DRY RED WINE

4 SHALLOTS, DICED

3 GARLIC CLOVES, MINCED

1 GREEN BELL PEPPER, STEMMED, SEEDED, AND DICED

1 RED, YELLOW, OR ORANGE BELL PEPPER, STEMMED, SEEDED, AND DICED

3 TABLESPOONS DRIED OREGANO

1 TABLESPOON GRANULATED GARLIC

1 TABLESPOON SUGAR

2 TABLESPOONS KOSHER SALT, PLUS MORE TO TASTE

½ TEASPOON RED PEPPER FLAKES

1 CUP WHITE RICE

BLACK PEPPER, TO TASTE

1 TABLESPOON CHOPPED FRESH OREGANO, FOR GARNISH

PARMESAN CHEESE, GRATED, FOR GARNISH

DIRECTIONS

1. Place all of the ingredients, except for the white rice, pepper, and the garnishes, in a slow cooker. Cook on low for 5½ hours.

2. Add the rice to the slow cooker, raise heat to high, and cook until the rice is tender, 40 to 50 minutes. The cooking time may vary depending on your slow cooker, so be sure to check after about 30 minutes to avoid overcooking the rice.

3. Season with salt and pepper, top with the oregano and a generous amount of Parmesan cheese, and serve.

Sesame Chicken with Blistered Shishito Peppers

YIELD: **4 SERVINGS**

ACTIVE TIME: **40 MINUTES**

TOTAL TIME: **1 HOUR AND 30 MINUTES**

Putting the Chinese takeout classic alongside the delicious and sporadically spicy shishito pepper is sure to produce plenty of smiles.

INGREDIENTS

FOR THE SESAME CHICKEN

2 TABLESPOONS OLIVE OIL, PLUS ½ TEASPOON

2" PIECE OF GINGER, PEELED AND SLICED

2 SCALLIONS, TRIMMED AND MINCED

2 GARLIC CLOVES, MINCED

JUICE OF ½ LEMON

4 BONELESS CHICKEN BREASTS

SALT AND PEPPER, TO TASTE

3 TABLESPOONS SESAME SEEDS

FOR THE SHISHITO PEPPERS

3 TABLESPOONS OLIVE OIL

1 LB. SHISHITO PEPPERS

SALT, TO TASTE

DIRECTIONS

1. To begin preparations for the chicken, place the 2 tablespoons of olive oil in a small skillet and warm over medium-high heat. When it starts shimmering, add the ginger, scallions, garlic, and lemon juice and sauté until the scallions are translucent, about 3 minutes. Remove from heat and transfer to a small bowl.

2. Season the chicken breasts with salt and pepper and put them in a resealable plastic bag. Add the ginger-and-scallion mixture and press it around the chicken breasts. Seal and let rest at room temperature for 30 minutes.

3. Preheat your gas or charcoal grill to medium-high heat. In a small dish, combine the remaining olive oil with the sesame seeds. Set aside.

4. When the grill is about 450°F, place the chicken on the grill and sprinkle the tops with half of the dressed sesame seeds. Grill the chicken breasts for about 7 minutes. Turn the chicken over, sprinkle the remaining sesame seeds on top, and grill until the breasts until they feel springy when poked, 5 to 6 minutes. Transfer to a plate and tent with aluminum foil to keep them warm.

5. To prepare the shishito peppers, place the olive oil in a large cast-iron skillet and warm over medium heat. When the oil is shimmering, add the peppers and cook, while turning once or twice, until they are blistered and golden brown all over, about 2 minutes. Transfer to a paper towel–lined plate, season with salt, and serve alongside the sesame chicken.

Chipotle Chicken Enchiladas

YIELD: **4 TO 6 SERVINGS**

ACTIVE TIME: **25 MINUTES**

TOTAL TIME: **1 HOUR AND 30 MINUTES**

Enchiladas are a wonderful meal for when you're not sure what you want to eat, as you can tailor them to your whims. This version utilizes a smoky, slightly spicy, dried chipotle sauce.

INGREDIENTS

FOR THE SAUCE

4 DRIED CHIPOTLE CHILI PEPPERS

½ (7 OZ.) CAN OF DICED MILD GREEN CHILIES

2 TABLESPOONS OLIVE OIL

2 TO 3 PLUM TOMATOES, SEEDED

1 TABLESPOON TOMATO PASTE

1 TABLESPOON CUMIN

1 TEASPOON DRIED OREGANO

SALT AND PEPPER, TO TASTE

FOR THE ENCHILADAS

¼ CUP OLIVE OIL (OR PREFERRED NEUTRAL OIL)

4 TO 6 BONELESS, SKINLESS CHICKEN THIGHS

SALT AND PEPPER, TO TASTE

2 CUPS CHICKEN STOCK (SEE PAGE 30 FOR HOMEMADE)

1 TO 2 RUSSET POTATOES, PEELED AND MINCED

Continued...

DIRECTIONS

1. To prepare the sauce, bring water to a boil in a small saucepan. Add the chipotles and cook until soft, about 10 minutes. Drain and transfer the chipotles to a blender or food processor. Add the remaining ingredients and puree until smooth. Add the puree to the skillet and cook over medium-low heat until the sauce is thick enough to coat the back of a spoon, about 15 to 20 minutes. Remove the sauce from the pan and set aside.

2. To begin preparations for the enchiladas, place a large cast-iron skillet over medium-high heat and warm 2 tablespoons of the oil in it. Season the chicken with salt and pepper and add it to the pan. Sear the chicken on both sides and then add 1½ cups of the chicken stock. Cover and cook until the chicken is tender enough to shred with a fork, about 20 minutes. Remove the chicken, transfer to a bowl, and shred with two forks.

3. Add the remaining oil and the potatoes to the skillet. Cook for 5 minutes, while stirring. Add the onion and garlic and cook until the onions start to soften, about 5 minutes. Stir often to avoid burning the vegetables.

4. Reduce heat to medium and add the shredded chicken, the remaining stock, the green chilies, and 1 tablespoon of the sauce. Cook until the chicken stock has evaporated, about 5 to 10 minutes. Remove the mixture from the pan and set it aside.

Continued...

½ WHITE ONION, MINCED

2 GARLIC CLOVES, MINCED

½ (7 OZ.) CAN OF DICED MILD GREEN CHILIES

16 TO 24 CORN TORTILLAS (SEE PAGE 68 FOR HOMEMADE)

1 CUP CRUMBLED COTIJA CHEESE, CRUMBLED, FOR GARNISH

CILANTRO, CHOPPED, FOR GARNISH

5. Preheat the oven to 375°F and grease a 9 x 13-inch baking pan with cooking spray. Place the tortillas on a work surface and spread a small amount of sauce on each of them. Evenly distribute the filling between the tortillas and roll them up. Place the tortillas seam-side down in the baking pan.

6. Top the enchiladas with the remaining sauce and place the pan in the oven. Bake for 20 minutes, or until a crust forms on the exterior of the tortillas. Garnish with the Cotija cheese and cilantro and serve.

YIELD: **6 SERVINGS**

ACTIVE TIME: **30 MINUTES**

TOTAL TIME: **3 HOURS AND 40 MINUTES**

Citrus & Sage Chicken with Golden Beets

This dish was made for the dead of winter, when citrus and root vegetables reach their sweetest point.

INGREDIENTS

FOR THE MARINADE

3 GARLIC CLOVES

⅓ CUP SAGE LEAVES

ZEST AND JUICE OF 1 ORANGE

1 TABLESPOON CORIANDER

½ TABLESPOON BLACK PEPPER

½ TEASPOON RED PEPPER FLAKES

¼ CUP OLIVE OIL

1 TABLESPOON KOSHER SALT

1 TABLESPOON MINCED SHALLOT

FOR THE CHICKEN & BEETS

6 BONE-IN, SKIN-ON CHICKEN THIGHS

2 LBS. GOLDEN BEETS, PEELED AND CUT INTO WEDGES

2 TABLESPOONS OLIVE OIL

SALT AND PEPPER, TO TASTE

1 CUP GRAPEFRUIT JUICE

4 LEEKS, WHITES ONLY, RINSED WELL, AND SLICED INTO THIN HALF-MOONS

1½ SHALLOTS, MINCED

4 TABLESPOONS UNSALTED BUTTER, CUT INTO 6 PIECES

DIRECTIONS

1. To prepare the marinade, place all of the ingredients in a blender and puree until smooth.

2. To begin preparations for the chicken and beets, place the chicken thighs in a resealable plastic bag, pour the marinade over the chicken thighs, and marinate in the refrigerator for 2 hours.

3. Preheat the oven to 375°F. Place the beets in a roasting pan, add the oil, season with salt and pepper, and toss to coat. Add the grapefruit juice, place the pan in the oven, and roast for 50 minutes.

4. Remove the pan from the oven, drain the grapefruit juice, and reserve it. Raise temperature to 400°F. Add the leeks and shallots to the pan and stir to combine. Push the vegetables to the outside of pan and nestle the chicken thighs, skin-side up, in the center. Place in the oven and cook for 40 minutes.

5. Remove the pan from the oven and pour the grapefruit juice over the chicken thighs. Turn the oven to the broiler setting. Place one piece of butter on each piece of chicken, place the pan under the broiler, and broil for 10 minutes, until the chicken is 165°F in the center. The beets should still have a slight snap to them, and the chicken's skin should be crispy. Remove and let cool briefly before serving.

Coconut Curry Chicken with Basmati Rice

The coconut milk tempers the spice just enough to ensure that your experience is pure pleasure.

INGREDIENTS

5 TABLESPOONS
GREEN CURRY PASTE

4 TO 6 BONELESS CHICKEN THIGHS

2 YELLOW ONIONS, PEELED
AND SLICED

2 CHILI PEPPERS, STEMMED,
SEEDED, AND SLICED

3 TABLESPOONS MASHED GINGER

1 GARLIC CLOVE, MASHED

3 TABLESPOONS FISH SAUCE

1 TABLESPOON MADRAS CURRY
POWDER

1 (14 OZ.) CAN OF COCONUT MILK

2 TABLESPOONS CHOPPED THAI
BASIL, PLUS MORE FOR GARNISH

1½ CUPS BASMATI RICE

1 CUP WATER

LIME WEDGES, FOR SERVING

CILANTRO, CHOPPED, FOR
GARNISH

DIRECTIONS

1. Preheat the oven to 375°F. Rub 2 tablespoons of the green curry paste on the chicken and set aside for at least 30 minutes. Place a cast-iron skillet over medium-high heat and add the chicken thighs, skin-side down. Cook until the skin is crispy, turn over, and cook for another 3 minutes. Remove the chicken from the skillet and set aside.

2. Add the onions, peppers, ginger, and garlic and cook, while stirring frequently and scraping the pan to remove any browned bits from the bottom, for 5 to 7 minutes.

3. When the vegetables are tender, add the remaining green curry paste and cook for an additional 3 minutes, until fragrant.

4. Add the fish sauce, Madras curry powder, coconut milk, and Thai basil and stir until combined. Add the rice and water, stir, and then return the chicken to the pan. Cover and transfer the pan to the oven. Bake until the rice is tender and has absorbed all of the liquid, about 25 minutes. Serve with the lime wedges and garnish with the additional Thai basil and cilantro.

Curried Chicken Salad with Apples & Pecans

YIELD: **6 SERVINGS**

ACTIVE TIME: **15 MINUTES**

TOTAL TIME: **45 MINUTES**

If you're one of those doing all they can to avoid carbs, serve this simple, flavor-packed salad over the baby arugula instead of on the marble rye.

INGREDIENTS

1½ LBS. BONELESS, SKINLESS CHICKEN BREASTS, CUT INTO ½" THICK CUTLETS

SALT AND PEPPER, TO TASTE

1 TABLESPOON OLIVE OIL

¼ CUP MAYONNAISE, PLUS MORE AS NEEDED

3 TABLESPOONS FRESH LIME JUICE

¼ CUP MADRAS CURRY POWDER

1 TABLESPOON CUMIN

1 TABLESPOON GRANULATED GARLIC

½ TEASPOON CINNAMON

½ TEASPOON TURMERIC

3 CELERY STALKS, MINCED

2 GRANNY SMITH APPLES, MINCED

½ RED BELL PEPPER, STEMMED, SEEDED, AND MINCED

¾ CUP PECANS, CHOPPED

5 TO 6 OZ. BABY ARUGULA

SLICES OF MARBLE RYE, TOASTED

DIRECTIONS

1. Preheat the oven to 350°F.

2. Place the chicken on a baking sheet. Season with salt and pepper and drizzle with the olive oil. Place the chicken in the oven and roast for 30 minutes, or until the center of the chicken reaches 160°F. Remove from the oven and let rest for 10 minutes.

3. Place the mayonnaise, lime juice, and all of the seasonings in a mixing bowl and stir to combine. Add the celery, apples, red pepper, and ½ cup of the pecans and stir to incorporate.

4. Once the chicken is cool enough to handle, dice into small cubes and add them to the bowl. Add the arugula and toss to combine. If the chicken salad is too dry for your liking, add mayonnaise as needed and stir to incorporate. Season to taste, top with the remaining pecans, and make sandwiches with the slices of marble rye.

Grilled Chicken Paninis with Sun-Dried Tomato Aioli

YIELD: **4 SERVINGS**

ACTIVE TIME: **30 MINUTES**

TOTAL TIME: **1 HOUR**

Constructing a delicious sandwich starts with quality bread. Once you've got that in place, the rest is easy.

INGREDIENTS

FOR THE AIOLI

1 CUP CHOPPED SUN-DRIED TOMATOES

1 CUP MAYONNAISE

1 TABLESPOON WHOLE GRAIN MUSTARD

2 TABLESPOONS CHOPPED FRESH PARSLEY

2 TABLESPOONS SLICED SCALLIONS

1 TEASPOON WHITE BALSAMIC VINEGAR

1 GARLIC CLOVE, MINCED

2 TEASPOONS KOSHER SALT

1 TEASPOON BLACK PEPPER

FOR THE SANDWICHES

8 SLICES OF CRUSTY WHITE BREAD

8 SLICES OF CHEDDAR CHEESE

4 (6 OZ.) GRILLED CHICKEN BREASTS

12 SLICES OF COOKED BACON

1 CUP ARUGULA

DIRECTIONS

1. Preheat a panini press.

2. To prepare the aioli, place all of the ingredients in a mixing bowl and stir until combined.

3. Spread some of the aioli on each slice of bread. Place a slice of cheddar on each slice of bread. Slice the chicken breasts and divide evenly between four pieces of the bread. Top the chicken with 3 slices of bacon and ¼ cup of the arugula. Assemble the sandwiches with the other slices of bread.

4. Place the sandwiches in the panini press and press until the cheese has melted and there is a nice crust on the bread. Remove and serve immediately.

NOTE: If you don't have a panini press, don't worry. Simply place 1 tablespoon of olive oil in a sauté pan and warm over medium-high heat. Place a sandwich in the pan, place a cast-iron skillet on top so it is pressing down on the sandwich, and cook until golden brown. Turn the sandwich over and repeat.

Chicken Vindaloo

A word of advice: add as much cayenne pepper as you and your family can handle, as this beloved preparation improves as it gets spicier.

YIELD: **6 SERVINGS**

ACTIVE TIME: **30 MINUTES**

TOTAL TIME: **2 HOURS AND 30 MINUTES**

INGREDIENTS

1 TABLESPOON GARAM MASALA

1 TEASPOON TURMERIC

2 TEASPOONS SWEET PAPRIKA

1 TEASPOON MUSTARD POWDER

2 TABLESPOONS SUGAR

1 TEASPOON CUMIN

½ TEASPOON CAYENNE PEPPER, OR TO TASTE

½ CUP RED WINE VINEGAR

¼ CUP TOMATO PASTE

5 TABLESPOONS OLIVE OIL

3 LBS. CHICKEN PIECES

1 LARGE YELLOW ONION, SLICED

6 GARLIC CLOVES, MINCED

1 TABLESPOON MINCED GINGER

1 (14 OZ.) CAN OF CHOPPED TOMATOES, DRAINED

FRESH CILANTRO, CHOPPED, FOR GARNISH

DIRECTIONS

1. Place the garam masala, turmeric, paprika, mustard powder, sugar, cumin, cayenne pepper, vinegar, tomato paste, and 2 tablespoons of the olive oil in a mixing bowl and stir to combine. Add the chicken to the mixture, turn until the pieces are evenly coated, cover the bowl, and place it in the refrigerator for at least 2 hours. If time allows, let the chicken marinate overnight.

2. Place a Dutch oven over high heat and add the remaining oil. When the oil starts to shimmer, add the onion and cook until it is translucent, about 3 minutes. Reduce the heat to medium, add the garlic and ginger, and sauté for 1 minute.

3. Add the tomatoes, chicken, and the marinade to the pot and bring to a boil. Reduce the heat and simmer until the chicken is cooked through, about 18 minutes. Garnish with the cilantro and serve.

Mojo Chicken

YIELD: **4 SERVINGS**

ACTIVE TIME: **30 MINUTES**

TOTAL TIME: **2 HOURS AND 30 MINUTES**

This fiery, Cuban-inspired dish will wake up your family's taste buds every time.

INGREDIENTS

1 YELLOW ONION, CHOPPED

10 GARLIC CLOVES, PEELED AND TRIMMED

2 SCOTCH BONNET PEPPERS, STEMMED, SEEDED, AND CHOPPED

1 CUP CHOPPED FRESH CILANTRO

1 TEASPOON DRIED THYME

1 TABLESPOON CUMIN

½ TEASPOON ALLSPICE

1 CUP ORANGE JUICE

½ CUP FRESH LEMON JUICE

½ TEASPOON CITRIC ACID

ZEST AND JUICE OF 1 LIME

¼ CUP OLIVE OIL

SALT AND PEPPER, TO TASTE

4 BONELESS, SKINLESS CHICKEN BREASTS

DIRECTIONS

1. Place all of the ingredients, except for the chicken, in a food processor or blender and puree until smooth. Reserve ½ cup of the marinade, pour the rest into a large resealable plastic bag, and add the chicken. Place in the refrigerator and marinate for at least 2 hours. If time allows, let the chicken marinate for up to 8 hours.

2. Remove the chicken from the refrigerator, remove it from the marinade, and pat dry. Preheat your gas or charcoal grill to medium-high heat.

3. When the grill is about 450°F, add the chicken and cook until both sides are charred and the breasts are cooked through, 4 to 5 minutes per side. The chicken breasts should be springy to the touch. Transfer the chicken to a plate and let sit for 10 minutes.

4. Place the reserved marinade in a saucepan and bring to a simmer over medium heat, until it starts to thicken, about 10 minutes. Spoon it over the chicken and serve immediately.

CHICKEN STOCK

Yield: 8 Cups   Active Time: 20 Minutes   Total Time: 6 Hours

7 lbs. chicken bones, rinsed

4 cups chopped yellow onions

2 cups chopped carrots

2 cups chopped celery

3 garlic cloves

3 sprigs of thyme

1 teaspoon black peppercorns

1 bay leaf

1. Place the chicken bones in a stockpot and cover with cold water. Bring to a simmer over medium-high heat and use a ladle to skim off any impurities that float to the top. Add the vegetables, thyme, peppercorns, and bay leaf, reduce the heat to low, and simmer for 5 hours, while skimming to remove any impurities that rise to the top.

2. Strain, allow to cool slightly, and transfer to the refrigerator. Leave uncovered and allow to cool completely. Remove layer of fat and cover. The stock will keep in the refrigerator for 3 to 5 days, and in the freezer for up to 3 months.

Shredded Chicken with Beans & Rice

YIELD: **6 SERVINGS**

ACTIVE TIME: **10 MINUTES**

TOTAL TIME: **5 TO 6 HOURS**

The cumin provides earthiness, the jalapeño provides a bit of heat, and they combine to add depth to what should be a simple bowl of chicken and rice.

INGREDIENTS

6 BONELESS, SKINLESS CHICKEN BREASTS

1 CUP CHICKEN STOCK (SEE SIDEBAR)

1 JALAPEÑO PEPPER, STEMMED, SEEDED, AND MINCED, PLUS MORE FOR GARNISH

2 GARLIC CLOVES, MINCED

1½ TABLESPOONS CUMIN

1 TABLESPOON GRANULATED GARLIC

1 CUP WHITE RICE

2 PLUM TOMATOES, DICED

2 TABLESPOONS KOSHER SALT

1 TABLESPOON BLACK PEPPER

1 (14 OZ.) CAN OF BLACK BEANS, DRAINED

DIRECTIONS

1. Place the chicken, stock, jalapeño, garlic, cumin, and granulated garlic in a slow cooker and cook on high until the chicken is very tender and falling apart, about 4 hours. Remove the chicken from the slow cooker, place it in a bowl, and shred it with a fork. Cover the bowl with aluminum foil and set it aside.

2. Add the rice, tomatoes, salt, and pepper to the slow cooker and cook until the rice is tender, 40 to 50 minutes. Make sure to check the rice after 30 minutes, since cook times will vary between different brands of slow cookers.

3. Add the black beans to the slow cooker, stir to combine, top with the shredded chicken, and cover until warmed through. Garnish with additional jalapeño and serve.

Jerk Chicken with Vegetables

YIELD: **6 SERVINGS**

ACTIVE TIME: **15 MINUTES**

TOTAL TIME: **24 HOURS**

By substituting root vegetables for the rice and beans that are traditionally served with jerk chicken, you add some nutrition to this delicious dish.

INGREDIENTS

FOR THE MARINADE

2 TABLESPOONS FRESH THYME LEAVES

2 HABANERO PEPPERS, STEMMED AND RIBS REMOVED, OR TO TASTE

½ YELLOW ONION

½ CUP BROWN SUGAR

½ TABLESPOON CINNAMON

½ TEASPOON NUTMEG

1 TABLESPOON ALLSPICE

2 TABLESPOONS MINCED FRESH GINGER

1 CUP OLIVE OIL

2 TABLESPOONS SOY SAUCE

1 SCALLION

1 TABLESPOON KOSHER SALT

1 TABLESPOON BLACK PEPPER

1 TABLESPOON RICE VINEGAR

Continued...

DIRECTIONS

1. To prepare the marinade, place all of the ingredients in a blender and blend until smooth.

2. To begin preparations for the chicken and vegetables, place the chicken in a large baking pan, pour the marinade over the chicken, and refrigerate overnight.

3. Preheat the oven to 375°F. Place the vegetables, oil, salt, and pepper in an 9 x 13-inch baking pan and roast for 30 minutes. Remove, add the thyme, return the pan to the oven, and roast for an additional 25 minutes. Remove the chicken from the refrigerator and let it come to room temperature.

4. Remove the pan from the oven. Shake the chicken to remove any excess marinade and then place the chicken on top of the vegetables. Return the pan to the oven and roast for 45 to 50 minutes, until the interiors of thickest parts of the chicken reach 165°F. Remove the pan from the oven and serve immediately.

FOR THE CHICKEN & VEGETABLES

5 LBS. BONE-IN, SKIN-ON CHICKEN
PIECES

3 RED BEETS, PEELED AND DICED

3 CARROTS, PEELED AND DICED

1 LARGE SWEET POTATO, PEELED
AND DICED

3 TURNIPS, PEELED AND DICED

¼ CUP OLIVE OIL

SALT AND PEPPER, TO TASTE

2 TABLESPOONS FRESH THYME
LEAVES, CHOPPED

SPATCHCOCKING

To spathcock a chicken or other bird, place it breast-side down on a cutting board and use a strong set of kitchen shears to cut along the backbone on each side. Remove the backbone, turn the bird over, and flatten the breastbone by pressing down with your hands.

Cider-Glazed Cornish Hens

This dish is perfect for a cool fall evening. Be sure to spatchcock the hens beforehand, as this will allow the breasts to cook evenly.

YIELD: **4 SERVINGS**

ACTIVE TIME: **40 MINUTES**

TOTAL TIME: **4 HOURS AND 30 MINUTES**

INGREDIENTS

FOR THE CORNISH HENS

4 CORNISH HENS, SPATCHCOCKED (SEE SIDEBAR)

SALT AND PEPPER, TO TASTE

¼ CUP OLIVE OIL

LEAVES FROM 1 SPRIG OF THYME

LEAVES FROM 1 SPRIG OF TARRAGON

1 TABLESPOON FRESH LEMON JUICE

FOR THE CIDER GLAZE

1 CUP SUGAR-FREE APPLE CIDER

1 TABLESPOON HONEY

4 TABLESPOONS UNSALTED BUTTER, CLARIFIED

FOR SERVING

MASHED POTATOES (OPTIONAL)

RICE PILAF (OPTIONAL)

DIRECTIONS

1. To begin preparations for the Cornish hens, season the Cornish hens with salt and pepper. Combine the olive oil, thyme, tarragon, and lemon juice in a small bowl and then place the Cornish hens in the mixture. Place in the refrigerator and marinate for 2 to 4 hours, turning the hens over every 30 minutes.

2. Remove the Cornish hens from the refrigerator and let them stand at room temperature. Preheat your gas or charcoal grill to medium heat and designate two separate heat sections on the grill, one for direct heat and the other for indirect. To do this, simply arrange the coals toward one side of a charcoal grill or turn off one of the burners on a gas grill.

3. To prepare the glaze, place all of the ingredients in a small saucepan and bring to a boil over medium-high heat. Cook until it has reduced to approximately ½ cup, about 10 minutes. Remove from heat and transfer to a small bowl.

4. When the grill is about 400°F, brush the Cornish hens with the glaze. Place the birds breast-side down over direct heat and cook for 3 minutes. When the skin is slightly crispy, turn the hens over and place over indirect heat. Cook for another 25 minutes, basting frequently with the remaining glaze, until the hens are cooked through.

5. Remove the hens from the grill and transfer to a large cutting board. Let rest for 10 minutes and serve with mashed potatoes or rice pilaf.

Korean Chicken Thighs with Sweet Potato Vermicelli

YIELD: **4 TO 6 SERVINGS**

ACTIVE TIME: **45 MINUTES**

TOTAL TIME: **3 HOURS AND 30 MINUTES**

The umami flavor of the sweet potato noodles, shiitake mushrooms, and cabbage is the perfect complement to the sweetness of the marinated chicken.

INGREDIENTS

FOR THE MARINADE

1 LEMONGRASS STALK, BOTTOM HALF ONLY

2 GARLIC CLOVES

1 TABLESPOON MINCED GINGER

1 SCALLION, TRIMMED

¼ CUP BROWN SUGAR

2 TABLESPOONS CHILI PASTE

1 TABLESPOON SESAME OIL

1 TABLESPOON RICE VINEGAR

2 TABLESPOONS FISH SAUCE

1 TABLESPOON BLACK PEPPER

FOR THE CHICKEN & VERMICELLI

4 TO 6 SKIN-ON, BONE-IN CHICKEN THIGHS

10 OZ. SWEET POTATO VERMICELLI

2 TABLESPOONS OLIVE OIL

2 TABLESPOONS SESAME OIL

Continued...

DIRECTIONS

1. To prepare the marinade, place all of the ingredients in a blender and blend until smooth.

2. To begin preparations for the chicken and vermicelli, place the chicken thighs in a large baking pan or resealable bag. Pour half of the marinade over the chicken thighs and marinate in the refrigerator for at least 2 hours. Set the rest of the marinade aside.

3. Remove the chicken from the refrigerator and let it come to room temperature. Fill a Dutch oven with water and bring to a boil. Add the vermicelli and cook until it is nearly al dente, about 6 minutes. Drain, rinse with cold water, and set aside.

4. Preheat the oven to 375°F. Remove the chicken from the refrigerator and place the Dutch oven on the stove. Add the olive oil and warm over medium-high heat. Remove the chicken thighs from the marinade and place them in the pot, skin-side down, until a crust forms on the skin, about 5 to 7 minutes. Turn the chicken thighs over, add the reserved marinade, place the pot in the oven, and roast for about 15 to 20 minutes, until the centers of the chicken thighs reach 165°F.

Continued...

2 CUPS CHOPPED NAPA CABBAGE

1 CUP SHIITAKE MUSHROOMS, SLICED THIN

1 SHALLOT, SLICED THIN

1 YELLOW ONION, SLICED THIN

2 GARLIC CLOVES, MINCED

2 TABLESPOONS MINCED GINGER

2 SCALLIONS, CHOPPED, GREENS RESERVED FOR GARNISH

¼ CUP BROWN SUGAR

2 TABLESPOONS FISH SAUCE

¼ CUP SOY SAUCE

¼ CUP RICE VINEGAR

¼ CUP SESAME SEEDS, FOR GARNISH

5. While the chicken thighs are roasting, place the sesame oil, cabbage, mushrooms, shallot, onion, garlic, scallion whites, and ginger in a skillet and cook over medium heat, stirring frequently, until the cabbage is wilted, about 6 minutes.

6. Place the brown sugar, fish sauce, soy sauce, and rice vinegar in a small bowl and stir until combined. Add this sauce and the vermicelli to the Dutch oven, stir until the noodles are coated, and then add the vegetable mixture to the pot. Top with the scallion greens and sesame seeds and return the pot to the oven for 5 minutes to warm through. Remove from the oven and serve immediately.

Chicken Thighs with Tabbouleh

YIELD: **4 SERVINGS**

ACTIVE TIME: **25 MINUTES**

TOTAL TIME: **1 HOUR**

Boneless, skinless chicken has made prep a lot simpler for many dishes, but for this preparation to reach maximum succulence, bones and skin are necessary.

INGREDIENTS

FOR THE CHICKEN THIGHS

2 TABLESPOONS OLIVE OIL

4 BONE-IN, SKIN-ON CHICKEN THIGHS

SALT AND PEPPER, TO TASTE

2 TEASPOONS PAPRIKA

2 TEASPOONS CUMIN

2 TEASPOONS GROUND FENNEL

1 CUP CHERRY TOMATOES

2 GARLIC CLOVES, CRUSHED

1 SHALLOT, SLICED

½ CUP WHITE WINE

Continued...

DIRECTIONS

1. To begin preparations for the chicken thighs, preheat the oven to 450°F. Place the olive oil in a cast-iron skillet and warm over medium-high heat. Sprinkle salt, pepper, the paprika, ground fennel, and cumin on the chicken thighs. When the oil starts to shimmer, place the thighs in the pan, skin-side down, and sear until browned. Turn the thighs over and place the pan in the oven. Roast until the internal temperature is 165°F, about 16 minutes. Halfway through, add the tomatoes, garlic, and shallot to the pan.

2. When chicken is fully cooked, remove the pan from the oven and transfer the chicken to a plate. Leave the vegetables in the pan, add the white wine, and place over high heat. Cook for 1 minute, while shaking the pan. Transfer the contents of the pan to the blender, puree until smooth, and season to taste. Set aside.

3. To prepare the tabbouleh, place the bulgur, water, shallot, thyme, and salt in a saucepan and bring to a boil. Remove from heat, cover the pan with foil, and let sit until the bulgur has absorbed all the liquid. Fluff with a fork, remove the shallot and thyme, and add the remaining ingredients. Season with salt and pepper and stir to combine.

4. To serve, place some of the tabbouleh on each plate. Top with a chicken thigh and spoon some of the puree over it.

FOR THE TABBOULEH

1 CUP BULGUR WHEAT

2 CUPS WATER

1 SHALLOT, HALVED

2 SPRIGS OF THYME

1 TABLESPOON KOSHER SALT, PLUS MORE TO TASTE

1 TABLESPOON CHOPPED CILANTRO

1 TABLESPOON CHOPPED PARSLEY

2 TABLESPOONS CHOPPED SCALLIONS

1½ TABLESPOONS FRESH LIME JUICE

½ CUP DICED TOMATO

½ CUP DICED CUCUMBER

1 GARLIC CLOVE, MINCED

3 TABLESPOONS OLIVE OIL

BLACK PEPPER, TO TASTE

Chicken & Tomatillo Casserole

YIELD: **6 SERVINGS**

ACTIVE TIME: **15 MINUTES**

TOTAL TIME: **24 HOURS**

Packed with shredded chicken and tangy tomatillos, this is what lasagna might have been had it been created in the Southwest.

INGREDIENTS

FOR THE MARINADE

1 TOMATILLO, HUSKED, RINSED, AND HALVED

1 PLUM TOMATO, HALVED

2 GARLIC CLOVES

1 SHALLOT, HALVED

1 POBLANO PEPPER, STEMMED, SEEDED, AND HALVED

¼ CUP OLIVE OIL

1 TABLESPOON KOSHER SALT

1 TABLESPOON CUMIN

FOR THE CASSEROLE

2 LBS. BONELESS, SKINLESS CHICKEN BREASTS, SLICED THIN

2 EGGS, BEATEN

1 (14 OZ.) CAN OF FIRE-ROASTED TOMATOES

PINCH OF KOSHER SALT

14 CORN TORTILLAS (SEE PAGE 68 FOR HOMEMADE)

SALSA VERDE (SEE SIDEBAR)

¼ CUP CRUMBLED COTIJA CHEESE

DIRECTIONS

1. To prepare the marinade, place all of the ingredients in a blender and puree until smooth.

2. To begin preparations for the casserole, place the chicken breasts in a large baking pan or resealable plastic bag. Pour the marinade over the chicken breasts and marinate in the refrigerator overnight.

3. Preheat the oven to 375°F. Place the chicken and marinade in a square 8" baking dish, place it in the oven, and roast until the center of the chicken reaches 165°F, about 30 minutes. Remove the dish from the oven, remove the chicken, transfer it to a mixing bowl, and shred it with a fork. Add the eggs, tomatoes, and salt to the bowl and stir to combine.

4. Place four of the tortillas in the baking dish. Add half of the chicken mixture, top with four more tortillas, and add the remaining chicken mixture. Top with the remaining tortillas, cover with the Salsa Verde, and then place the dish in the oven. Bake for about 30 minutes, until the center is hot. Remove, sprinkle the cheese on top, and return to the oven. Bake until the cheese has melted, remove, and serve.

SALSA VERDE

Yield: 1 Cup   Active Time: 5 Minutes   Total Time: 15 Minutes

6 tomatillos, husked and rinsed

8 serrano peppers, stemmed and seeded, ribs removed to taste

½ yellow onion

2 garlic cloves

Salt, to taste

½ cup olive oil

Cilantro, chopped, for garnish

1. Place the tomatillos and serrano peppers in a large saucepan and cover with water. Bring to a boil and cook until the tomatillos start to lose their bright green color, about 10 minutes.

2. Drain and transfer the tomatillos and peppers to a blender. Add all of the remaining ingredients, except for the cilantro, and puree until smooth. Top with the cilantro and serve. The salsa will keep in the refrigerator for up to 2 days.

Chicken Kebabs

This recipe is simply one of the best, and easiest, ways to make the most of chicken thighs.

YIELD: **4 SERVINGS**

ACTIVE TIME: **20 MINUTES**

TOTAL TIME **2 HOURS AND 30 MINUTES**

INGREDIENTS

2 TABLESPOONS PAPRIKA

1 TEASPOON TURMERIC

1 TEASPOON ONION POWDER

1 TEASPOON GARLIC POWDER

1 TABLESPOON DRIED OREGANO

¼ CUP OLIVE OIL, PLUS MORE AS NEEDED

2 TABLESPOONS WHITE WINE VINEGAR

1 CUP PLAIN GREEK YOGURT

1 TEASPOON KOSHER SALT, PLUS MORE TO TASTE

3 LBS. BONELESS, SKINLESS CHICKEN THIGHS, CUT INTO BITE-SIZED PIECES

BLACK PEPPER, TO TASTE

LEMON WEDGES, FOR SERVING

DIRECTIONS

1. Place the paprika, turmeric, onion powder, garlic powder, oregano, olive oil, vinegar, yogurt, and salt in a large bowl and whisk to combine. Add the chicken pieces and stir until they are coated. Cover the bowl, place it in the refrigerator, and let the chicken marinate for at least 2 hours. If you have time, you can also let the chicken marinate overnight.

2. Remove the chicken from the refrigerator and let it sit at room temperature for about 30 minutes.

3. Preheat your gas or charcoal grill to medium-high heat or place a cast-iron grill pan or skillet over medium-high heat and warm for 10 minutes. While the grill or the pan is heating up, thread the chicken onto the skewers and season with salt and pepper.

4. Brush the grill or the pan with a light coating of olive oil and then add the chicken kebabs. Cook, turning occasionally, until the chicken is golden brown and cooked through, approximately 10 minutes. Serve warm or at room temperature with the lemon wedges.

Chicken Fajitas

YIELD: **6 SERVINGS**

ACTIVE TIME: **30 MINUTES**

TOTAL TIME: **5 HOURS**

The trick is to bring this dish to the table while the meat and veggies are still sizzling, as the sound is sure to get tongues wagging.

INGREDIENTS

FOR THE CHICKEN

½ CUP ORANGE JUICE

JUICE OF 1 LIME

4 GARLIC CLOVES, MINCED

1 JALAPEÑO PEPPER, STEMMED, SEEDED, AND CHOPPED

2 TABLESPOONS CHOPPED FRESH CILANTRO

1 TEASPOON CUMIN

1 TEASPOON DRIED OREGANO

SALT AND PEPPER, TO TASTE

3 TABLESPOONS OLIVE OIL

4 BONELESS, SKINLESS CHICKEN BREASTS, CUT INTO STRIPS

FOR THE VEGETABLES

2 TABLESPOONS OLIVE OIL

1 RED ONION, SLICED THIN

1 RED BELL PEPPER, STEMMED, SEEDED, AND SLICED THIN

1 GREEN BELL PEPPER, STEMMED, SEEDED, AND SLICED THIN

1 YELLOW BELL PEPPER, STEMMED, SEEDED, AND SLICED THIN

Continued...

DIRECTIONS

1. To begin preparations for the chicken, place the orange juice, lime juice, garlic, jalapeño, cilantro, cumin, oregano, salt, and pepper in a bowl and stir to combine. When thoroughly combined, add the olive oil. Add the chicken pieces to the mixture, stir until they are evenly coated, cover with plastic wrap, and refrigerate for about 4 hours.

2. Remove the chicken from the refrigerator and let it come to room temperature.

3. Place a 12" cast-iron skillet over medium-high heat. Add the chicken and cook, while stirring, until browned and cooked through, about 8 minutes. Transfer the chicken to a bowl and tent with aluminum foil to keep warm.

4. To prepare the vegetables, reduce the heat to medium, add the olive oil to the skillet, and then add the onion, peppers, and garlic. Cook, while stirring, until the vegetables have softened, about 5 minutes. Add the lime juice and cilantro, season with salt and pepper, and cook until the vegetables are tender, about 10 minutes.

5. Push the vegetables to one side of the pan and put the chicken on the other side. Serve immediately with the tortillas and Pico de Gallo.

2 JALAPEÑO PEPPERS, STEMMED,
SEEDED, AND SLICED THIN

3 GARLIC CLOVES, MINCED

¼ CUP FRESH LIME JUICE

½ CUP CHOPPED FRESH CILANTRO

SALT AND PEPPER, TO TASTE

FOR SERVING

CORN TORTILLAS (SEE PAGE 68
FOR HOMEMADE)

PICO DE GALLO (SEE SIDEBAR)

PICO DE GALLO

4 plum tomatoes, chopped

1 jalapeño pepper, chopped

½ cup chopped red onion

¼ cup chopped fresh cilantro

Zest and juice of ½ lime

Salt, to taste

1. Place all of the ingredients in a mixing bowl and stir to combine. Refrigerate for 1 hour before serving to let the flavors mingle.

SOFRITO

Yield: 2 Cups   Active Time: 10 Minutes   Total Time: 10 Minutes

2 poblano peppers, stemmed and seeded

1 white onion, peeled and cut into quarters

1 red bell pepper, stemmed and seeded

1 green bell pepper, stemmed and seeded

3 plum tomatoes

2 garlic cloves

1 tablespoon cumin

2 tablespoons adobo seasoning

1. Dice 1 of the poblanos, half of the onion, and half of each of the bell peppers. Place the rest of the ingredients in a blender or food processor and puree until smooth. Add the diced vegetables, stir to combine, and serve.

Puerto Rican Rice & Beans

YIELD: **6 SERVINGS**

ACTIVE TIME: **15 MINUTES**

TOTAL TIME: **1 HOUR AND 45 MINUTES**

This is the perfect recipe to serve at a large family gathering. And, as this gets even better the next day, don't hesitate to whip up a double batch.

INGREDIENTS

½ LB. KIDNEY BEANS, SOAKED OVERNIGHT AND DRAINED

¼ CUP OLIVE OIL

4 BONELESS, SKINLESS CHICKEN THIGHS

2 PIECES SALT PORK, MINCED (ABOUT 4 OZ.)

1 CUP SOFRITO (SEE SIDEBAR)

1 CUP SPANISH-STYLE TOMATO SAUCE, PUREED

2 CUPS WHITE RICE

3 TO 3½ CUPS CHICKEN STOCK (SEE PAGE 30 FOR HOMEMADE)

2 PACKETS OF SAZÓN WITH ACHIOTE

2 TABLESPOONS DRIED OREGANO

1 CUP SPANISH OLIVES WITH THE BRINE

ADOBO SEASONING, TO TASTE

DIRECTIONS

1. Place the beans in a Dutch oven and cover with water. Bring to a boil, reduce heat to medium-low, and cover the pot. Cook until the beans are tender, 45 minutes to 1 hour. Drain and set the beans aside.

2. Place the pot back on the stove and add half of the oil. Add the chicken and cook over medium-high heat for 5 minutes on each side. Remove the chicken from the Dutch oven, cut it into 12 pieces, and set aside.

3. Add the salt pork and the remaining oil to the pot and cook until some of the salt pork's fat has rendered, about 5 minutes. Add the Sofrito and the tomato sauce. Cook for 5 minutes, stirring constantly.

4. Add the rice to the pot, stir, and cook for 5 minutes. Add the remaining ingredients and return the chicken to the pot. Reduce heat to medium and cook for 10 minutes. Cover the Dutch oven and cook until the liquid has been absorbed and the rice is tender, 20 to 30 minutes.

5. Uncover the pot and add the beans. Stir to combine and serve.

Buffalo Wings

YIELD: **4 SERVINGS**

ACTIVE TIME: **30 MINUTES**

TOTAL TIME: **45 MINUTES**

The classic we all know and love, now in the comfort of your home.

INGREDIENTS

4 TABLESPOONS UNSALTED BUTTER

1 TABLESPOON WHITE VINEGAR

¾ CUP HOT SAUCE

1 TEASPOON CAYENNE PEPPER (OPTIONAL)

4 CUPS VEGETABLE OIL

2 LBS. CHICKEN WINGS

1 CUP CORNSTARCH

SALT, TO TASTE

BLUE CHEESE DRESSING (SEE SIDEBAR), FOR SERVING

CELERY STICKS, FOR SERVING

DIRECTIONS

1. Place the butter in a Dutch oven and warm over medium heat. When it has melted, whisk in the vinegar, hot sauce, and cayenne (if using), making sure not to breathe in the spicy steam. Transfer the sauce to a mixing bowl and cover to keep warm.

2. Wipe out the Dutch oven, add the vegetable oil, and slowly bring it to 375°F over medium heat. While the oil is heating, pat the chicken wings dry and, working in batches, toss them in the cornstarch.

3. Add the coated wings to the oil in batches and fry until they are crispy, about 10 minutes. Transfer the cooked wings to a wire rack and season with salt. Add the cooked wings to the spicy sauce, toss to coat, and serve them with the Blue Cheese Dressing and celery sticks.

BLUE CHEESE DRESSING

¼ cup sour cream

¼ cup mayonnaise

¼ cup buttermilk

1 tablespoon fresh lemon juice

Pinch of black pepper

1 cup crumbled blue cheese

1. Place the sour cream, mayonnaise, buttermilk, lemon juice, and pepper in a bowl and whisk to combine.

2. Add the blue cheese and stir to incorporate. The dressing will keep in the refrigerator for up to 1 week.

TIP: If you are looking for a spot to utilize the duck fat you reserved in this preparation, use it in place of oil the next time you roast potatoes. It will add a crisp exterior that gives way to a fluffy, flavorful inside.

Thai Red Duck Curry

YIELD: **4 SERVINGS**

ACTIVE TIME: **15 MINUTES**

TOTAL TIME: **30 MINUTES**

Your local grocery store will likely have precooked duck breasts available for purchase, but it's worth cooking your own just to have access to the rich, rendered fat that results from searing them.

INGREDIENTS

4 SKIN-ON DUCK BREASTS

¼ CUP THAI RED CURRY PASTE

2½ CUPS COCONUT MILK

10 MAKRUT LIME LEAVES (OPTIONAL)

1 CUP DICED PINEAPPLE

1 TABLESPOON FISH SAUCE, PLUS MORE TO TASTE

1 TABLESPOON BROWN SUGAR

6 BIRD'S EYE CHILI PEPPERS, STEMMED, SEEDED, AND MINCED

20 CHERRY TOMATOES

1 CUP BASIL (THAI BASIL STRONGLY PREFERRED)

1½ CUPS COOKED JASMINE RICE, FOR SERVING

DIRECTIONS

1. Use a very sharp knife to slash the skin on the duck breasts, while taking care not to cut all the way through to the meat.

2. Place a Dutch oven over medium-high heat. Place the duck breasts, skin-side down, in the pot and sear until browned, about 4 minutes. This will render a lot of the fat.

3. Turn the duck breasts over and cook until browned on the other side, about 4 minutes. Remove the duck from the pot, let cool, and drain the rendered duck fat. Reserve the duck fat for another use.

4. When the duck breasts are cool enough to handle, remove the skin and discard. Cut each breast into 2" pieces.

5. Turn heat to medium, add the curry paste to the Dutch oven, and fry for 2 minutes. Add the coconut milk, bring to a boil, and cook for 5 minutes.

6. Reduce the heat, return the duck to the pot, and simmer for 8 minutes. Add the pineapple, fish sauce, brown sugar, and chilies, stir to incorporate, and simmer for 5 minutes. Skim to remove any fat from the top as the curry simmers.

7. Taste and add more fish sauce if needed. Stir in the cherry tomatoes and basil and serve over rice.

Chicken Tsukune

YIELD: **4 TO 6 SERVINGS**

ACTIVE TIME: **10 MINUTES**

TOTAL TIME: **20 MINUTES**

Rich chicken thighs are essential here, as they ensure that the result is juicy and deeply flavorful. Make these ahead for a party or serve as part of a Japanese-themed dinner with miso soup and seaweed salad.

INGREDIENTS

2 LBS. CHICKEN THIGH MEAT, GROUND

1 LARGE EGG, LIGHTLY BEATEN

1 CUP PANKO BREAD CRUMBS

2 TEASPOONS MISO

2 TABLESPOONS SAKE

1½ TABLESPOONS MIRIN

½ TEASPOON BLACK PEPPER

TARE SAUCE (SEE SIDEBAR)

1½ SCALLIONS, TRIMMED AND SLICED, FOR GARNISH

SESAME SEEDS, FOR GARNISH

DIRECTIONS

1. Place the ground chicken, egg, panko bread crumbs, miso, sake, mirin, and the pepper in a bowl and stir to combine. Cover the bowl and place it in the refrigerator while you make the sauce.

2. When the sauce has been prepared, remove the chicken mixture from the refrigerator and form it into compact pieces that are round or oblong.

3. Place a cast-iron grill pan over high heat and lightly coat with nonstick cooking spray.

4. When the pan is hot, add the meatballs and cook until they start to brown, about 3 minutes. Turn over and cook until they are completely cooked through, about 4 minutes. Remove from the pan and lightly baste the cooked meatballs with the Tare Sauce.

5. Garnish the meatballs with the sesame seeds and scallions and serve alongside the remaining Tare Sauce.

TIP: For a different presentation, thread the meatballs on skewers before adding them to the pan or placing them on a grill.

TARE SAUCE

½ cup chicken stock (see page 30 for homemade)

½ cup soy sauce

½ cup mirin

¼ cup sake

½ cup brown sugar

2 garlic cloves, smashed

1" piece of ginger, peeled and sliced

1½ scallions, sliced

1. Place the ingredients in a small saucepan and bring to a simmer over low heat. Simmer for 10 minutes, stirring once or twice.

2. Remove from heat, let cool, and strain before using.

Five-Spice Turkey Breast

Proof that turkey isn't just for the holidays, and doesn't need to be flanked by a number of rich sides. When searching for something to round out the plate, keep it simple: potatoes, rice, or a salad.

YIELD: **4 SERVINGS**

ACTIVE TIME: **30 MINUTES**

TOTAL TIME: **2 HOURS**

INGREDIENTS

2 TABLESPOONS CHINESE FIVE-SPICE POWDER

1 TEASPOON CINNAMON

1 TABLESPOON BROWN SUGAR

1 TEASPOON BLACK PEPPER

1 BONE-IN, SKIN-ON WHOLE TURKEY BREAST

2 TABLESPOONS OLIVE OIL

DIRECTIONS

1. Preheat the oven to 375°F.

2. Place the five-spice powder, cinnamon, brown sugar, and pepper in a small bowl and stir to combine.

3. Pat the turkey breast dry with paper towels and coat it liberally with the spice mixture.

4. Place the oil in a 12" cast-iron skillet and warm over medium heat. When the oil starts to shimmer, add the turkey, skin-side down, and sear until it is browned, about 5 minutes.

5. Carefully turn the turkey over, cover the pan, and place in the oven for 1½ hours.

6. Remove the pan from the oven and let the turkey rest for 15 minutes.

7. Place the turkey breast on a cutting board, remove the bone, slice, and serve.

TIP: You can also let the turkey cool down completely after removing it from the oven and make sandwiches on French bread with lots of shredded cabbage, carrots, and cilantro.

CHAPTER 2

BEEF

The rich, mouthwatering sight of just-cooked red meat begs for a marriage of seasonings that will bring out the subtle flavors resting within. While some will swear that beef needs nothing more than salt and pepper, the marinade utilized in the Carne Asada (see pages 68–69) or the rub and sauce that enliven the Coffee & Bourbon Brisket (see pages 60–61) prove that those folks are terribly shortsighted.

A magical transformation takes place when a cut of beef is paired with bold seasonings and long prep times, be it marinating in the refrigerator or braising in a Dutch oven. When that combination of daring and patience is present, dinner becomes an event.

Chili con Carne

YIELD: **6 SERVINGS**

ACTIVE TIME: **30 MINUTES**

TOTAL TIME: **3 TO 4 HOURS**

Save this for a Sunday during football season: it's so good, it won't even matter if your team ends up losing.

INGREDIENTS

1½ LBS. GROUND BEEF

1 (28 OZ.) CAN OF CRUSHED SAN MARZANO TOMATOES

1 RED BELL PEPPER, DICED

2 SMALL YELLOW ONIONS, DICED, PLUS MORE FOR GARNISH

3 TO 4 GARLIC CLOVES, MINCED

1 JALAPEÑO PEPPER, STEMMED AND MINCED

1 LB. PINK BEANS, SOAKED OVERNIGHT AND DRAINED

¼ CUP CHOPPED FRESH CILANTRO, PLUS MORE FOR GARNISH

¼ CUP HOT SAUCE

2 TABLESPOONS CHILI POWDER

1 TABLESPOON BLACK PEPPER

1 TABLESPOON KOSHER SALT

2 TABLESPOONS GRANULATED GARLIC

⅓ CUP CUMIN

1 TABLESPOON MADRAS CURRY POWDER

1 TABLESPOON DRIED OREGANO

CHEDDAR CHEESE, GRATED, FOR GARNISH

DIRECTIONS

1. Place the ground beef in a Dutch oven and cook, while breaking it up with a wooden spoon, over medium heat until it is browned.

2. Drain off the fat, add all of the remaining ingredients, except for the garnishes, and stir to combine. Bring to a boil, reduce heat so that the chili gently simmers, and cook until the beans are fork-tender and the flavor is to your liking, 3 to 4 hours. Ladle into warmed bowls and garnish with the cheddar cheese, and the additional onion and cilantro.

NOTE: If you aren't a fan of spice, remove the ribs from the jalapeño, or just omit it entirely.

DRY RUB

Yield: About 1 Cup   Active Time: 5 Minutes   Total Time: 5 Minutes

¼ cup ground coffee

1 teaspoon ground coriander

2 teaspoons black pepper

Pinch of red pepper flakes

1 teaspoon cumin

2 teaspoons mustard powder

2 teaspoons dark chili powder

1 teaspoon paprika

6 tablespoons kosher salt

6 tablespoons light brown sugar

1. Place all of the ingredients in a mixing bowl and stir to combine. Transfer the mixture to an airtight container and store for up to 6 months.

Coffee & Bourbon Brisket

YIELD: **6 SERVINGS**

ACTIVE TIME: **15 MINUTES**

TOTAL TIME: **8 HOURS AND 30 MINUTES**

You'll learn to love this marriage of Texas and Southern BBQ, where the slight bitterness of coffee and sweet bourbon work beautifully together.

INGREDIENTS

FOR THE BRISKET

1 YELLOW ONION, DICED

1 PEACH, PEELED, PITTED, AND DICED

1 NECTARINE, PEELED, PITTED, AND DICED

2 TABLESPOONS MINCED GINGER

½ CUP DRY RUB (SEE SIDEBAR)

3½ LBS. FLAT-CUT BRISKET

1 CUP WATER

FOR THE COFFEE & BOURBON BBQ SAUCE

2 CUPS BREWED COFFEE

¼ CUP DARK BROWN SUGAR

¾ CUP BOURBON

3 TABLESPOONS MOLASSES

¼ CUP RAW APPLE CIDER VINEGAR

2 TABLESPOONS WORCESTERSHIRE SAUCE

¼ CUP KETCHUP

1 TABLESPOON GRANULATED GARLIC

½ TABLESPOON BLACK PEPPER, COARSELY GROUND

1 TABLESPOON TAPIOCA STARCH OR CORNSTARCH

DIRECTIONS

1. To prepare the brisket, place the onion, peach, nectarine, and ginger in a slow cooker. Apply the Dry Rub to the brisket and place the brisket on top of the mixture in the slow cooker. Add the water, cover, and cook on low for 6 hours.

2. Remove the contents of the slow cooker, transfer the brisket to a cutting board, and discard everything else. Place all of the ingredients for the BBQ sauce in the slow cooker and cook on high for 1 hour.

3. Return the brisket to the slow cooker, reduce the heat to low, and cook for another hour. Remove the brisket from the slow cooker, let rest for 30 minutes, and then use a sharp knife to cut it into ½" slices against the grain.

Chimichurri Strip Steak with Oregano Potatoes & Onions

A classic Argentinian meal that requires nothing more than a simple salad of tomatoes, cucumbers, greens, and onions for company.

YIELD: **4 SERVINGS**

ACTIVE TIME: **20 MINUTES**

TOTAL TIME: **24 HOURS**

INGREDIENTS

FOR THE SAUCE

2 TABLESPOONS FRESH OREGANO

¼ CUP OLIVE OIL

2 CUPS FRESH PARSLEY

1½ CUPS FRESH CILANTRO

1 SMALL YELLOW ONION, CHOPPED

2 SCALLIONS, TRIMMED

1 JALAPEÑO PEPPER, STEMMED AND RIBS REMOVED, OR TO TASTE

1 TEASPOON KOSHER SALT

1 TEASPOON BLACK PEPPER

1 TEASPOON ONION POWDER

1 TEASPOON GARLIC POWDER

1 TABLESPOON SUGAR

⅓ CUP WATER

FOR THE STEAK, POTATOES & ONIONS

4 (5 TO 6 OZ.) N.Y. STRIP STEAKS

Continued...

DIRECTIONS

1. To prepare the sauce, place all of the ingredients in a blender and puree until smooth. Transfer half of the sauce and the steaks to an airtight container and let them marinate in the refrigerator overnight. Refrigerate the other half of the sauce in a separate container.

2. Preheat the oven to 375°F.

3. Remove the steaks from the marinade and season both sides with salt. Set aside and let come to room temperature as you cook the potatoes and onions.

4. Place the sweet potatoes, the potatoes, and salt in a large cast-iron skillet. Cover with water, bring to a boil, and cook until the potatoes are tender, about 20 minutes. Drain and set aside.

5. Wipe the pan, add the olive oil and beef tallow, and warm over medium-high heat. When the oil starts to shimmer, add the steaks and cook for 2 minutes on each side. Remove the steaks from the pan and set aside.

6. Place the sweet potatoes, potatoes, onion, and 3 tablespoons of the reserved chimichurri sauce in the pan and cook, stirring continuously, over medium heat until the onion is soft, about 10 minutes. Add the vinegar, wine, and oregano and cook until the vinegar and wine have nearly evaporated, about 5 minutes.

Continued...

SALT AND PEPPER, TO TASTE

1 LB. WHITE SWEET POTATOES, PEELED AND DICED

1 LB. YUKON GOLD POTATOES, PEELED AND DICED

1 TABLESPOON OLIVE OIL

2 TABLESPOONS BEEF TALLOW

1 LARGE WHITE ONION, SLICED THIN

¼ CUP RED WINE VINEGAR

⅓ CUP DRY RED WINE

1 TABLESPOON CHOPPED FRESH OREGANO

7. Return the steaks to the pan and place it in the oven for 5 minutes. Remove the pan from the oven, divide between serving plates, top with the remaining chimichurri sauce, and serve with a small salad.

TIP: Beef tallow is the rendered fat of beef, and a great substitute for butter. If you are feeling adventurous and want the authentic taste for this dish, you can ask your local butcher where to purchase it. You can also ask him for some beef fat, grind it in a food processor until fine, and cook it in a slow cooker on low for 6 to 8 hours. Then strain the fat through a coffee filter and store the liquid in the refrigerator until ready to use. To get 1 cup of tallow you'll need 1 pound of beef fat.

DASHI BROTH

Yield: 6 Cups   Active Time: 10 Minutes   Total Time: 1 Hour

8 cups cold water   1 cup bonito flakes

2 oz. kombu

1. Place the water and the kombu in a saucepan. Soak for 20 minutes, remove the kombu, and score it gently with a sharp knife.

2. Return the kombu to the saucepan and bring the water to a boil. Remove the kombu as soon as the water boils, so that the broth doesn't become bitter. Add the bonito flakes and return to a boil. Turn off the heat and let the broth stand for 25 minutes.

3. Strain through a fine sieve and chill the stock, uncovered, in the refrigerator. Cover when it has cooled completely and store in the refrigerator for up to 1 week and in the freezer for up to 3 months.

Sukiyaki

YIELD: **4 SERVINGS**

ACTIVE TIME: **5 MINUTES**

TOTAL TIME: **15 MINUTES**

This modest Japanese preparation will quickly become a family favorite.

INGREDIENTS

SALT, TO TASTE

1½ LBS. UDON NOODLES

1 TABLESPOON OLIVE OIL

3 TABLESPOONS BROWN SUGAR

2 LBS. RIB EYE, SLICED VERY THIN

½ CUP MIRIN

½ CUP SAKE

⅓ CUP SOY SAUCE

1 CUP DASHI BROTH (SEE SIDEBAR) OR WATER

1 BUNCH OF SCALLIONS, SLICED INTO 2" PIECES

2 CUPS CHOPPED NAPA CABBAGE

1 BUNCH OF ENOKI MUSHROOMS

6 LARGE SHIITAKE MUSHROOMS

1 CUP FRESH SPINACH

½ LB. TOFU, DRAINED AND CUT INTO ¼" CUBES

DIRECTIONS

1. Bring salted water to a boil in a Dutch oven. Add the noodles to the boiling water and cook for 2 minutes. Drain, rinse with cold water, and set the noodles aside.

2. Place the olive oil in the Dutch oven and warm over medium-high heat. When the oil starts to shimmer, add the brown sugar and steak and cook, while turning, until the steak is browned all over, about 2 minutes. Add the mirin, sake, soy sauce, and Dashi Broth or water and stir to combine.

3. Carefully arrange the noodles, scallions, cabbage, mushrooms, spinach, and tofu in the broth. Cover and steam until the cabbage is wilted, about 5 minutes. Ladle into warmed bowls and serve immediately.

Pho

YIELD: **4 SERVINGS**

ACTIVE TIME: **15 MINUTES**

TOTAL TIME: **4 TO 8 HOURS**

This is a fairly traditional pho, but don't be afraid to be bold with your additions, as the possible variations are almost endless.

INGREDIENTS

FOR THE BROTH

8 CUPS BEEF STOCK (SEE SIDEBAR)

1 LARGE CINNAMON STICK

4 BAY LEAVES

6 STAR ANISE PODS

2 TEASPOONS KOSHER SALT

2 TEASPOONS PEPPERCORNS

2 TEASPOONS CORIANDER SEEDS

1 TEASPOON ALLSPICE BERRIES

1 TEASPOON FENNEL SEEDS

¼ CUP SMASHED FRESH GINGER

6 GARLIC CLOVES, SMASHED

4 LEMONGRASS STALKS, BRUISED

1 WHITE ONION, CUT INTO 6 WEDGES

2 TABLESPOONS DARK SOY SAUCE

2 TABLESPOONS RICE VINEGAR

2 TABLESPOONS FISH SAUCE

FOR THE NOODLES & STEAK

½ LB. RICE NOODLES

4 BABY BOK CHOY, WASHED AND QUARTERED

Continued...

DIRECTIONS

1. To prepare the broth, place all of the ingredients in a slow cooker, cover, and cook on low for at least 4 hours. For a very flavorful broth, cook for 8 hours.

2. Strain the broth through a fine sieve. Discard the solids and return the broth to the slow cooker. To begin preparations for the noodles and steak, add the noodles and bok choy to the broth, cover, and cook on low for approximately 30 minutes, until the noodles are tender and the bok choy is al dente.

3. Slice the steak into ⅛" thick pieces. Ladle the broth, noodles, and bok choy into bowls and top with the steak. The broth will cook the steak to rare. If you prefer the steak to be cooked more, add the slices to the slow cooker and cook in the broth for 2 to 3 minutes for medium-rare, and 3 to 5 minutes for medium. Season with Sriracha. If desired, garnish with bean sprouts, chili peppers, Thai basil, and/or scallions, and serve with lime wedges.

1½ LBS. N.Y. STRIP STEAK

SRIRACHA, TO TASTE

FOR GARNISH & SERVING

1½ CUPS BEAN SPROUTS
(OPTIONAL)

2 CHILI PEPPERS, SLICED
(OPTIONAL)

CILANTRO, WASHED AND TORN
(OPTIONAL)

THAI BASIL LEAVES, CHOPPED
(OPTIONAL)

SCALLIONS, CHOPPED (OPTIONAL)

LIME WEDGES (OPTIONAL)

BEEF STOCK

Yield: 8 Cups   Active Time: 20 Minutes
Total Time: 6 Hours

---

7 lbs. beef bones, rinsed	3 garlic cloves, crushed
4 cups chopped yellow onions	3 sprigs of thyme
2 cups chopped carrots	1 teaspoon black peppercorns
2 cups chopped celery	1 bay leaf

1. Place the beef bones in a stockpot and cover with cold water. Bring to a simmer over medium-high heat and use a ladle to skim off any impurities that float to the top. Add the vegetables, thyme, peppercorns, and bay leaf, reduce the heat to low, and simmer for 5 hours, while skimming to remove any impurities that rise to the top.

2. Strain, allow to cool slightly, and transfer to the refrigerator. Leave uncovered and allow to cool completely. Remove layer of fat and cover. The stock will keep in the refrigerator for 3 to 5 days, and in the freezer for up to 3 months.

CORN TORTILLAS

Yield: 20 Tortillas   Active Time: 40 Minutes   Total Time: 40 Minutes

---

2 cups masa harina, plus more as needed

½ teaspoon kosher salt

1 cup warm water (105°F), plus more as needed

2 tablespoons vegetable oil

1.   Place the masa harina and salt in a bowl and stir to combine. Slowly add the warm water and oil and stir until they are incorporated and a soft dough forms. The dough should be quite soft but not at all sticky,. If it is too dry, add more water. If the dough is too wet, add more masa harina. Wrap the dough in plastic and let it rest at room temperature for 30 minutes. It can also be stored in the refrigerator for up to 24 hours.

2.   Warm a cast-iron skillet over medium-high heat. Pinch off a small piece of dough and roll it into a ball. Place the ball between two pieces of parchment paper or plastic wrap and using large cookbook (or something of similar weight) to flatten the ball into a thin disk.

3.   Place the disk in the skillet and cook until brown spots begin to appear, about 45 seconds. Flip the disk over, cover for 1 minute, and transfer the cooked tortilla to a plate. Cover with a kitchen towel and repeat the remaining dough.

Carne Asada

YIELD: **4 SERVINGS**

ACTIVE TIME: **30 MINUTES**

TOTAL TIME: **3 HOURS**

Most people make this on the grill, but even direct flame cannot equal the power of a cast-iron skillet here.

INGREDIENTS

1 JALAPEÑO PEPPER, STEMMED, SEEDED, AND MINCED

3 GARLIC CLOVES, MINCED

½ CUP CHOPPED FRESH CILANTRO

¼ CUP OLIVE OIL, PLUS MORE AS NEEDED

JUICE OF 1 SMALL ORANGE

2 TABLESPOONS APPLE CIDER VINEGAR

2 TEASPOONS CAYENNE PEPPER

1 TEASPOON ANCHO CHILI POWDER

1 TEASPOON GARLIC POWDER

1 TEASPOON PAPRIKA

1 TEASPOON KOSHER SALT

1 TEASPOON CUMIN

1 TEASPOON DRIED OREGANO

¼ TEASPOON BLACK PEPPER

2 LBS. FLANK OR SKIRT STEAK, TRIMMED

CORN TORTILLAS (SEE SIDEBAR), FOR SERVING

DIRECTIONS

1. Place all of the ingredients, except for the steak and the tortillas, in a baking dish or a large resealable plastic bag and stir to combine. Add the steak, place in the refrigerator, and let marinate for at least 2 hours. If time allows, marinate the steak overnight.

2. Approximately 30 minutes before you are going to cook the steak, remove it from the marinade, pat it dry, and let it come to room temperature.

3. Place a 12" cast-iron skillet over high heat and add enough oil to coat the bottom. When the oil starts to shimmer, add the steak and cook on each side for 6 minutes for medium-rare.

4. Remove the steak from the pan and let rest for 5 minutes before slicing it into thin strips, making sure to cut against the grain. Serve with tortillas and your favorite taco toppings.

Steak with Peppers & Onions

YIELD: **4 SERVINGS**

ACTIVE TIME: **20 MINUTES**

TOTAL TIME: **2 HOURS AND 30 MINUTES**

If you somehow end up with leftovers, put them on a crusty roll with some arugula.

INGREDIENTS

½ CUP OLIVE OIL

2 GARLIC CLOVES, MINCED

2 TEASPOONS WORCESTERSHIRE SAUCE

2 TEASPOONS RED WINE VINEGAR

1 TABLESPOON MUSTARD POWDER

2 LBS. SIRLOIN TIPS, CUT INTO BITE-SIZED PIECES

2 YELLOW ONIONS, CHOPPED

2 RED BELL PEPPERS, STEMMED, SEEDED, AND CHOPPED

SALT AND PEPPER, TO TASTE

DIRECTIONS

1. Place 7 tablespoons of the oil in a large bowl. Add the garlic, Worcestershire sauce, red wine vinegar, and mustard powder and stir to combine. Add the sirloin tips and stir until they are coated. Cover and refrigerate for at least 2 hours, while stirring once or twice. If time allows, let the meat marinate overnight.

2. Approximately 30 minutes before you are ready to cook, remove the sirloin tips from the marinade and allow them to come to room temperature.

3. Place a 12" cast-iron skillet over medium-high heat and coat the bottom with the remaining oil. When it starts to shimmer, add the sirloin tips and cook until they are browned all over, about 8 minutes. Remove from the pan and set aside.

4. Reduce heat to medium, add the onions and peppers, and cook, without stirring, until they start to brown, about 5 minutes. Return the sirloin tips to the pan and cook for an additional 2 minutes. Season with salt and pepper and serve immediately.

TOASTED RICE POWDER

Yield: ½ Cup   Active Time: 5 Minutes   Total Time: 10 Minutes

½ cup jasmine rice

1. Warm a cast-iron skillet over medium-high heat. Add the rice and toast until it starts to brown.

2. Remove and grind into a fine powder using a mortar and pestle.

Crying Tiger Beef

YIELD: **4 SERVINGS**

ACTIVE TIME: **15 MINUTES**

TOTAL TIME: **30 MINUTES**

Don't be thrown by the name—the only tears resulting from this dish are those of joy.

INGREDIENTS

2 LBS. FLANK STEAK

2 TABLESPOONS SOY SAUCE

1 TABLESPOON OYSTER SAUCE

1 TABLESPOON BROWN SUGAR, PLUS 1 TEASPOON

1 LARGE TOMATO, SEEDED AND DICED

⅓ CUP FRESH LIME JUICE

¼ CUP FISH SAUCE

2 TABLESPOONS MINCED FRESH CILANTRO

1½ TABLESPOONS TOASTED RICE POWDER (SEE SIDEBAR)

1 TABLESPOON RED PEPPER FLAKES

1 CUP SOFT HERB LEAF MIX (MINT, BASIL, AND CILANTRO), FOR GARNISH

DIRECTIONS

1. Place the steak in a bowl and add the soy sauce, oyster sauce, and the 1 tablespoon of brown sugar. Stir to combine and then let the steak marinate for 10 minutes.

2. Place a 12" cast-iron skillet over high heat and spray it with nonstick cooking spray. Add the steak and cook until medium, about 5 minutes per side. Transfer to a plate, cover with foil, and let rest for 5 minutes before slicing into thin strips, making sure to cut across the grain.

3. Place the tomato, lime juice, fish sauce, remaining brown sugar, cilantro, Toasted Rice Powder, and red pepper flakes in a bowl and stir to combine. The powder won't dissolve, but it will lightly bind the rest of the ingredients together. Divide the dipping sauce between the serving bowls. Top with the slices of beef and garnish each portion with the soft herb leaf mix.

TIP: If you're able to track it down, Thai holy basil will take this dish up another level.

Sichuan Cumin Beef

YIELD: **4 SERVINGS**

ACTIVE TIME: **10 MINUTES**

TOTAL TIME: **1 HOUR AND 15 MINUTES**

This extremely fragrant recipe possesses equally heady flavors thanks to the unique buzz the Sichuan peppercorn supplies.

INGREDIENTS

3 TABLESPOONS CUMIN SEEDS

2 TEASPOONS SICHUAN PEPPERCORNS

1 TEASPOON KOSHER SALT

3 TABLESPOONS OLIVE OIL

4 WHOLE DRIED RED CHILI PEPPERS

2 TEASPOONS RED PEPPER FLAKES

1½ LBS. CHUCK STEAK, CUT INTO 1" PIECES

1 YELLOW ONION, SLICED

2 SCALLIONS, TRIMMED AND SLICED THIN, FOR GARNISH

½ CUP CHOPPED FRESH CILANTRO, FOR GARNISH

DIRECTIONS

1. Place the cumin seeds and Sichuan peppercorns in a dry skillet and toast over medium heat until they are fragrant, about 1 minute. Do not let them burn. Remove and grind to a fine powder with a mortar and pestle.

2. Place the salt, 2 tablespoons of the oil, the dried chilies, red pepper flakes, and the toasted spice powder into a large bowl and stir to combine. Add the chuck steak and toss until coated. Cover with a kitchen towel and let stand for 1 hour.

3. Warm a skillet over high heat until the pan is extremely hot. Add the remaining oil, swirl to coat, and then add the steak and onion. Cook, stirring occasionally, until the beef is browned all over, about 10 minutes. Garnish with the scallions and cilantro and serve immediately.

Papas Rellenas

These crispy, stuffed potato balls are a classic of Cuban cuisine.

YIELD: **4 TO 6 SERVINGS**

ACTIVE TIME: **30 MINUTES**

TOTAL TIME: **1 HOUR**

INGREDIENTS

3 LBS. POTATOES, PEELED AND CHOPPED

1 GARLIC CLOVE, MINCED

2 TEASPOONS KOSHER SALT

1 TEASPOON BLACK PEPPER

1 TABLESPOON VEGETABLE OIL, PLUS MORE FOR FRYING

1 SMALL GREEN BELL PEPPER, SEEDED AND MINCED

1 YELLOW ONION, MINCED

½ LB. GROUND BEEF

2 TABLESPOONS TOMATO PASTE

¼ CUP PITTED AND MINCED GREEN OLIVES

¼ CUP RAISINS

½ TEASPOON PAPRIKA

2 EGGS, LIGHTLY BEATEN

½ CUP BREAD CRUMBS

DIRECTIONS

1. Bring water to a boil in a large saucepan. Add the potatoes, cover the pan, and cook until fork-tender, about 25 minutes. Drain the potatoes, place them in a large bowl, and mash until smooth. Add the garlic and half of the salt and pepper and stir to incorporate.

2. Warm the vegetable oil in a skillet over medium heat. When the oil starts to shimmer, add the bell pepper and onion and cook until the onion is translucent, about 3 minutes. Add the ground beef and cook, while breaking it up with a wooden spoon, until it is browned, about 10 minutes. Add the tomato paste, olives, raisins, paprika, and the remaining salt and pepper and cook for 2 minutes. Transfer the mixture to a paper towel–lined baking sheet and let it drain.

3. Add vegetable oil to a Dutch oven until it is 2" deep and bring it to 375°F. Place the eggs and bread crumbs in two separate bowls. Place 2 tablespoons of the potato mixture in one hand, pat it flat, and then place a tablespoon of the ground beef mixture in the center. Shape the potato around the filling to create a ball and dip the ball into the egg. Roll the ball in the bread crumbs until coated and place on a parchment-lined baking sheet. Repeat until all of the potato mixture and ground beef mixture have been used up.

4. Place the balls in the hot oil and cook until golden brown, about 2 minutes. Remove with a slotted spoon and set them on a paper towel–lined plate to drain. When all of the balls have been fried, serve with your favorite condiments.

Momos

The meat of choice in Tibet, where these dumplings are beloved, is yak, but ground beef will also work.

YIELD: **4 SERVINGS**

ACTIVE TIME: **45 MINUTES**

TOTAL TIME: **1 HOUR AND 30 MINUTES**

INGREDIENTS

¾ LB. GROUND BEEF

3 GARLIC CLOVES, MINCED

½ LARGE YELLOW ONION, MINCED

5 SCALLION WHITES, SLICED THIN

2" PIECE OF GINGER, PEELED AND MINCED

SALT, TO TASTE

¾ TEASPOON SICHUAN PEPPERCORNS

2 TABLESPOONS SAFFLOWER OR PEANUT OIL

5 TABLESPOONS WATER

30 DUMPLING WRAPPERS

CABBAGE LEAVES, FOR STEAMING

GINGERY RED PEPPER SAUCE (SEE SIDEBAR), FOR SERVING

DIRECTIONS

1. Place the ground beef, garlic, onion, scallion whites, ginger, and a couple pinches of salt in a mixing bowl and stir to combine. Place the Sichuan peppercorns in a small dry skillet and toast over medium heat until fragrant, 2 to 3 minutes. Using a spice grinder or a mortar and pestle, crush the peppercorns into a fine powder. Place the powder in a bowl, add the oil, water, and a couple of pinches of salt and stir to combine. Pour over the ground beef mixture and stir to incorporate.

2. Place a wrapper in a cupped hand and place about 1 tablespoon of filling in the center, leaving about ¾" of open wrapper around the edge. Moisten the edge with a wet finger, fold into a half-moon, and press down to seal, trying to remove as much air as possible. To pleat the sealed edge, make small folds in the wrapper and press them flat as you work along the edge. Place the sealed dumpling on a parchment-lined baking sheet and repeat with the remaining wrappers and filling.

3. Place 1" of water in a large pot and bring it to a boil. Line a steaming tray with the cabbage leaves and then add the momos in batches, leaving ½" between each of the dumplings and also between the dumplings and the edge of the tray. Place the steaming tray over the boiling water, cover, and steam until the dumplings have puffed up slightly and become slightly translucent, about 8 minutes. Transfer to a warmed plate, tent loosely with foil to keep warm, and repeat with the remaining dumplings. Serve immediately with the Gingery Red Pepper Sauce.

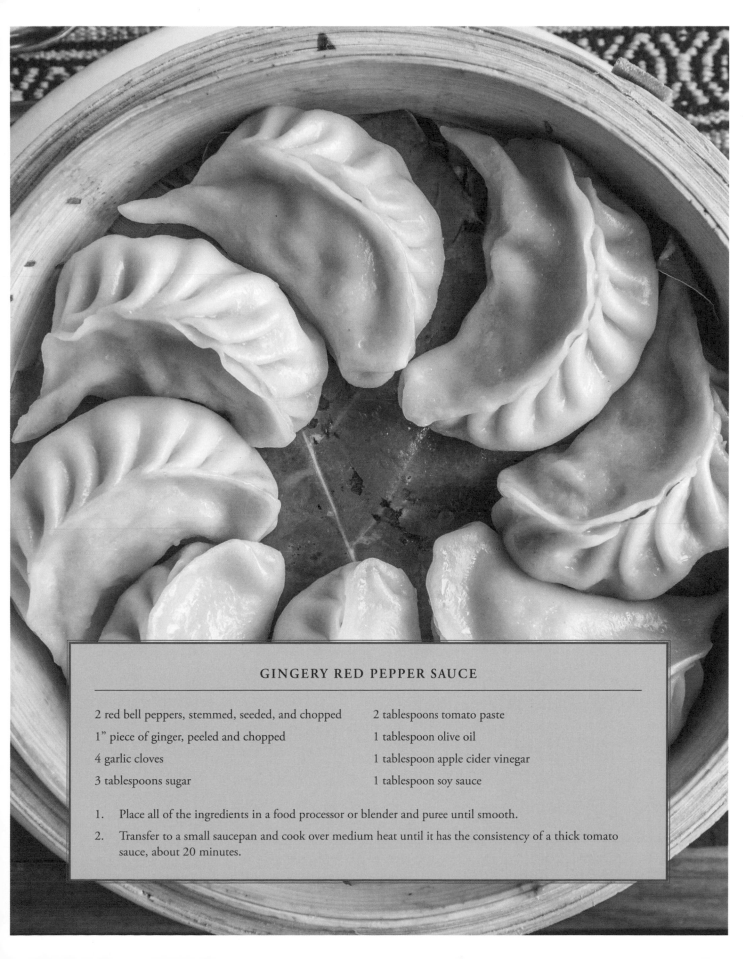

GINGERY RED PEPPER SAUCE

2 red bell peppers, stemmed, seeded, and chopped

1" piece of ginger, peeled and chopped

4 garlic cloves

3 tablespoons sugar

2 tablespoons tomato paste

1 tablespoon olive oil

1 tablespoon apple cider vinegar

1 tablespoon soy sauce

1. Place all of the ingredients in a food processor or blender and puree until smooth.

2. Transfer to a small saucepan and cook over medium heat until it has the consistency of a thick tomato sauce, about 20 minutes.

Kibbeh bil Sanieh

YIELD: **4 SERVINGS**

ACTIVE TIME: **20 MINUTES**

TOTAL TIME: **1 HOUR AND 20 MINUTES**

If you're unfamiliar, kibbeh is a deeply flavorful Levantine dish consisting of ground meat, bulgur, and onions. This version leans heavily on the smoky depth of Aleppo pepper, but if you can't track it down, red pepper flakes will do.

INGREDIENTS

2 TABLESPOONS OLIVE OIL

1 LARGE YELLOW ONION, MINCED

1½ LBS. GROUND BEEF

½ CUP PINE NUTS

2 TEASPOONS ALLSPICE

2 CUPS BULGUR WHEAT, RINSED

1 TABLESPOON TOMATO PASTE

1 TABLESPOON ALEPPO PEPPER

1 TABLESPOON KOSHER SALT, PLUS MORE TO TASTE

LEMON WEDGES, FOR SERVING

DIRECTIONS

1. Preheat the oven to 350°F.

2. Place half of the oil in a large skillet and warm over medium heat. When it is shimmering, add half of the onion and sauté until translucent, about 3 minutes. Add two-thirds of the ground beef and cook, while stirring, until lightly browned, about 8 minutes. Transfer the meat-and-onion mixture to a bowl, add the pine nuts and half of the allspice, and stir to combine. Set the mixture aside.

3. Place the remaining beef, onion, and allspice in a food processor with the bulgur, tomato paste, Aleppo peper, and salt. Pulse until it is a paste.

4. Grease a cast-iron skillet and cover the bottom of the pan with the meat-and-bulgur paste. Press down to create an even layer. Top with the meat-and-pine nut mixture and score it in a diamond pattern. Drizzle the remaining oil over the top and place the skillet in the oven. Bake for 1 hour, until the bulgur is tender. Season with salt and serve with the lemon wedges.

INGREDIENTS

3 LBS. SIRLOIN

6 TABLESPOONS OLIVE OIL

3 TABLESPOONS RED WINE VINEGAR

JUICE OF 2 LEMONS

2 TEASPOONS CINNAMON

2 TABLESPOONS CORIANDER

1 TABLESPOON BLACK PEPPER

1 TEASPOON CARDAMOM

1 TEASPOON GROUND CLOVES

½ TEASPOON MACE

PINCH OF GROUND NUTMEG

1 TABLESPOON GARLIC POWDER

2 YELLOW ONIONS, SLICED INTO THIN HALF-MOONS

SALT, TO TASTE

1 TEASPOON SUMAC POWDER

1 CUP PLAIN GREEK YOGURT, FOR SERVING

PITA BREAD, FOR SERVING

2 PERSIAN CUCUMBERS, DICED, FOR SERVING

2 ROMA TOMATOES, DICED, FOR SERVING

½ CUP FRESH MINT LEAVES, TORN, FOR SERVING

Beef Shawarma

The secret ingredient in this dish is sumac, a popular spice in Middle Eastern cuisine that adds a beguiling sourness. This is typically served in a pita to be eaten on the go, but is just as nice out on the patio with friends and a light cucumber salad.

DIRECTIONS

1. Place sirloin in the freezer for 30 minutes so that it will be easier to slice. After 30 minutes, use an extremely sharp knife to slice it as thin as possible.

2. Place the sirloin in a large mixing bowl. Add the olive oil, vinegar, lemon juice, cinnamon, coriander, pepper, cardamom, cloves, mace, nutmeg, and garlic powder and stir to combine. Place in the refrigerator and let it marinate for 1 hour. If you have time, let the meat marinate overnight for even more flavor.

3. Place the sliced onions in a baking dish and cover with water. Add a pinch of salt and several ice cubes. Place in the refrigerator for at least 30 minutes and up to 4 hours.

4. Remove the meat from the refrigerator and let it come to room temperature. Drain the onions, squeeze to remove any excess water, and place them in a bowl. Add the sumac powder and toss to coat. Set aside.

5. Warm a cast-iron grill pan over high heat. When it is warm, add the meat in batches and cook, while turning, until it is browned all over.

6. To serve, place a dollop of yogurt on a pita and top with some of the meat, onions, cucumbers, tomatoes, and mint leaves.

Steak au Poivre

When making this French classic, keep in mind that you'll get the best results from the best ingredients. If at all possible, go to a top local farm for the meat, shallots, chives, and cream.

YIELD: **4 SERVINGS**

ACTIVE TIME: **40 MINUTES**

TOTAL TIME: **2 HOURS**

INGREDIENTS

4 (½ LB.) N.Y. STRIP STEAKS

SALT, TO TASTE

2 TABLESPOONS BLACK PEPPERCORNS

1 TABLESPOON OLIVE OIL

2 TABLESPOONS UNSALTED BUTTER, CUT INTO SMALL PIECES

4 SMALL SHALLOTS, MINCED

⅔ CUP COGNAC

1 CUP HEAVY CREAM

SPRIGS OF ROSEMARY, FOR GARNISH (OPTIONAL)

DIRECTIONS

1. Preheat the oven to 200°F and place an oven-safe platter on one of the racks.

2. Pat the steaks dry and season both sides with salt.

3. Place the peppercorns in a resealable plastic bag and, working on a hard, flat surface, crush them with a meat tenderizer or mallet. Pour them onto a plate and press both sides of the steaks into them, distributing peppercorns evenly over the meat.

4. Place a 12" cast-iron skillet over medium-high heat for 5 minutes. Add the oil and swirl to coat the bottom of the pan. Put the steaks in the pan and sear on both sides, cooking for about 3 minutes per side for medium-rare.

5. Transfer steaks to the platter in the oven. Reduce heat to medium, add a tablespoon of the butter to the skillet, let it melt, and add the shallots. As they sauté, scrape up the browned bits stuck to the bottom of the pan. Cook until the shallots are browned, about 5 minutes. Pour the Cognac in the pan and use a long-handled lighter to ignite it. The flame will subside in a minute or so. Cook the sauce until it is nearly boiling, while stirring constantly.

6. Add the cream and any juices from the platter the steaks are on. Reduce the heat and cook the sauce until it has reduced, about 5 minutes. Stir in the last tablespoon of butter. Put the steaks on a plate and pour the sauce over them. Garnish with rosemary, if desired, and serve.

Rib Eye with Salsa Verde & Porcini Mushroom Salt

YIELD: **4 SERVINGS**

ACTIVE TIME: **30 MINUTES**

TOTAL TIME: **1 HOUR AND 15 MINUTES**

This is not the tomatillo-based salsa verde that most know, but the parsley-based version beloved by Italians.

INGREDIENTS

2 (1 LB.) BONE-IN RIB EYES, TRIMMED

1 TEASPOON KOSHER SALT, PLUS MORE TO TASTE

BLACK PEPPER, TO TASTE

2 TABLESPOONS CANOLA OIL

1 CUP DRIED PORCINI MUSHROOMS, MINCED

½ CUP OLIVE OIL

2 TABLESPOONS CAPERS

2 GARLIC CLOVES

1 TEASPOON LEMON ZEST

1 CUP FRESH FLAT-LEAF PARSLEY

DIRECTIONS

1. Preheat a gas or charcoal grill to 425°F. Season the steaks with salt and pepper and let them stand at room temperature for 30 minutes.

2. Brush the grill grates with the canola oil, place the steaks on the grill, and cook until charred, about 6 minutes. Turn the steaks over and cook until they are charred and slightly springy to the touch, 6 to 8 minutes. Remove the steaks from the grill, transfer to a platter, and tent it loosely with aluminum foil. Let the steaks rest for 10 minutes.

3. Place the dried mushrooms and the teaspoon of salt in a small bowl and stir to combine. Set the porcini mushroom salt aside.

4. Place half of the olive oil, the capers, garlic, lemon zest, and parsley in a food processor and pulse until a paste forms. Transfer the salsa verde to a bowl, stir in the remaining olive oil, and season to taste with salt and pepper. Serve the steaks with the salsa verde and the porcini mushroom salt.

Marinated Short Ribs

YIELD: **4 TO 6 SERVINGS**

ACTIVE TIME: **20 MINUTES**

TOTAL TIME: **8 HOURS**

Short rib is an inexpensive and underutilized cut that packs plenty of flavor when correctly prepared. This marinade helps you do precisely that.

INGREDIENTS

FOR THE MARINADE

2 CUPS BASIL LEAVES, MINCED

2 LARGE CARROTS, PEELED AND MINCED

2 LARGE YELLOW ONIONS, MINCED

2 GARLIC CLOVES, MINCED

1 SCALLION, TRIMMED AND MINCED

LEAVES FROM 2 SPRIGS OF THYME

LEAVES FROM 2 SPRIGS OF ROSEMARY

LEAVES FROM 2 SPRIGS OF OREGANO

3 TABLESPOONS OLIVE OIL

1 (750 ML) BOTTLE OF DRY RED WINE

FOR THE SHORT RIBS

3 TO 4 LBS. BEEF SHORT RIBS, CUT INTO 4" PIECES

SALT AND PEPPER, TO TASTE

DIRECTIONS

1. To prepare the marinade, place all of the ingredients, except for the wine, in a large bowl or roasting pan. Add the short ribs and then add the wine. Transfer the bowl to the refrigerator and marinate for 4 to 6 hours.

2. Remove the short ribs from the marinade, place them on a large cutting board or plate, and let stand at room temperature for 1 hour. Season one side of the ribs with salt and pepper.

3. Preheat your gas or charcoal grill to medium-high heat.

4. Once the grill is 450°F, place the ribs on the grill, seasoned-side down, and cook for about 4 minutes. Season the tops of the ribs with salt and pepper as they cook. When the ribs are charred, flip them over and cook for 4 more minutes. The short ribs will be medium-rare.

5. Transfer the ribs to a cutting board and let rest for 5 to 10 minutes before serving.

CHAPTER 3

PORK

No other meat stands up to high and low temperatures better than pork.
Whether you're searing a tenderloin or braising a pork belly,
pork offers some of the juiciest preparations in this entire book.
It is truly one of the most forgiving meats.

From this humble protein spring some of the world's most decadent
dishes, as demonstrated by the Porchetta (see page 111) and
Pork with Blue Cheese Polenta & Roasted Peach Hot Sauce (see pages
104–105). But, as the Spicy Tonkatsu (see page 92) and Bulgogi
with Musaengchae (see pages 112–113) show, it can also shine
when speed and simplicity are called for.

Spicy Tonkatsu

A spicy take on a beloved Japanese dish.

YIELD: **4 SERVINGS**

ACTIVE TIME: **30 MINUTES**

TOTAL TIME: **30 MINUTES**

INGREDIENTS

1½ LBS. PORK CUTLETS

¼ CUP WASABI PASTE

¼ CUP OLIVE OIL

2 TABLESPOONS HORSERADISH

1 TABLESPOON MINCED PARSLEY

2 TABLESPOONS MINCED CHIVES

SALT AND PEPPER, TO TASTE

2 CUPS PANKO BREAD CRUMBS

LEMON WEDGES, FOR SERVING

DIRECTIONS

1. Preheat the broiler on your oven. Pat the cutlets dry and lightly coat each one with the wasabi paste. In a bowl, combine 2 tablespoons of the olive oil, the horseradish, parsley, chives, salt, and pepper. Add the bread crumbs and carefully stir to coat. Set the seasoned panko aside.

2. Place a 12" cast-iron skillet over medium heat and coat the bottom with the remaining olive oil. When the oil is shimmering, add the pork cutlets and cook until golden brown, about 5 minutes. Flip the cutlets over and cook until golden brown on the other side.

3. Remove the cutlets from the skillet and dip each one into the seasoned panko until completely coated. Return the coated cutlets to the skillet. While keeping a close watch, place the pan under the broiler. Broil, turning the cutlets over once, until the crust is browned and crispy. Slice and serve with the lemon wedges.

Maple & Mustard Pork Tenderloin

YIELD: **6 SERVINGS**

ACTIVE TIME: **20 MINUTES**

TOTAL TIME: **1 HOUR AND 30 MINUTES**

Oven-roasted pork helps keep the blues away when the cold weather comes. The sweetness of the maple syrup in this dish doesn't hurt either.

INGREDIENTS

2 LBS. RED POTATOES, CUT INTO WEDGES

2 YELLOW ONIONS, CUT INTO ½" THICK SLICES

4 CELERY STALKS, CUT INTO 5" PIECES

½ LB. CARROTS, WASHED AND HALVED LENGTHWISE

3 TABLESPOONS OLIVE OIL

SALT AND PEPPER, TO TASTE

2½ LBS. PORK TENDERLOIN

¼ CUP REAL MAPLE SYRUP

5 GARLIC CLOVES, MINCED

1 CUP CHICKEN STOCK (SEE PAGE 30 FOR HOMEMADE)

3 BAY LEAVES

DIRECTIONS

1. Preheat the oven to 375°F. In a 9 x 13-inch baking pan, place the potatoes, onions, celery, and carrots. Add 2 tablespoons of the olive oil, season with salt and pepper, and toss to coat. Cover the pan with foil and roast in the oven for 30 minutes.

2. While the vegetables are cooking, rub the tenderloin with the maple syrup and the remaining olive oil. Season with salt and pepper and let the pork come to room temperature.

3. Remove the pan from the oven, remove the foil, and set aside. Add the garlic, stock, and bay leaves. Place the tenderloin on top of the vegetables and return the pan to the oven. Roast for 45 to 50 minutes, or until the center of the pork reaches 145°F. Cooking times will vary in different ovens, so make sure you check the pork after 30 minutes.

4. Remove the pan from the oven and transfer the pork to a cutting board. Place the reserved foil over it and let the pork rest for 10 to 15 minutes.

5. Remove the carrots, celery, 1 cup of the onions, and the juices from the pan. Transfer to a blender and puree until smooth. Remember to vent the blender slightly so that the steam can escape.

6. Slice the tenderloin into 1" thick pieces. Place the potatoes and remaining onions on the serving plates and top with the pork and sauce.

INGREDIENTS

FOR THE BBQ SAUCE

½ CUP KETCHUP

¼ CUP DARK BROWN SUGAR

2 TABLESPOONS GRANULATED SUGAR

2 TABLESPOONS DIJON MUSTARD

3 TABLESPOONS APPLE CIDER VINEGAR

2 GARLIC CLOVES, MINCED

¼ CUP BLACKSTRAP MOLASSES

¼ TEASPOON GROUND CLOVES

½ TEASPOON HOT SAUCE

¼ CUP HONEY

FOR THE RIBS

10 LBS. ST. LOUIS-CUT PORK RIBS

½ CUP KOSHER SALT

2 TABLESPOONS LIGHT BROWN SUGAR

2 TABLESPOONS GARLIC POWDER

1 TABLESPOON ONION POWDER

1 TABLESPOON CHILI POWDER

1 TABLESPOON PAPRIKA

1 TABLESPOON CUMIN

2 CUPS APPLEWOOD CHIPS

8 CUPS APPLE JUICE OR APPLE CIDER

Applewood-Smoked Ribs with Molasses BBQ Sauce

The St. Louis cut, which removes the rib tips, sternum, and cartilage, ensures that the ribs cook evenly.

DIRECTIONS

1. To prepare the BBQ sauce, place all of the ingredients in a medium saucepan and bring to a boil over medium-high heat. Reduce heat so that the sauce simmers and cook, stirring occasionally, for 20 minutes. Remove pan from heat and set aside.

2. To begin preparations for the ribs, place the ribs in a roasting pan. Place all of the remaining ingredients, except for the wood chips and the apple juice or apple cider, in a bowl and stir until combined.

3. Rub the mixture in the bowl all over the ribs, making sure every inch is covered. Place the ribs in the refrigerator for 1 hour.

4. Heat your smoker to 250°F and place the BBQ sauce beside it. Once it reaches the desired temperature, add the applewood chips and 1 cup of apple juice or cider to the steam tray. Place the ribs in the smoker and cook, while brushing the ribs with the sauce every 30 minutes, for about 4 hours, until the meat begins to pull away from the bones. While the ribs are cooking, make sure you keep an eye on the steam tray and continue refilling it with apple juice or cider. You do not want the steam tray to be dry for any length of time.

5. When the ribs have finished cooking, remove them from the smoker, wrap in foil, and let rest for 20 minutes before serving.

NOTE: *If you do not have a smoker, you can still prepare this dish on your grill. Soak the applewood chips in apple juice or apple cider for 1 hour before grilling and either place them on the coals or, if using a gas grill, into a smoker box before placing the ribs on the grill.*

Peppered Pork Shoulder with Apples, Carrots & Onions

YIELD: **4 TO 6 SERVINGS**

ACTIVE TIME: **20 MINUTES**

TOTAL TIME: **6 HOURS**

This dish is heavenly on a crisp night with warm bread and a glass of dry hard cider.

INGREDIENTS

1 LB. BABY RAINBOW CARROTS, HALVED LENGTHWISE

5 CELERY STALKS, CUT INTO 4" PIECES

2 TO 3 LARGE YELLOW ONIONS, QUARTERED

2 GRANNY SMITH APPLES, CORED AND CUT INTO WEDGES

3½-LB. BONE-IN PORK SHOULDER

1 CINNAMON STICK

4 TO 5 GARLIC CLOVES, CRUSHED

1 TABLESPOON KOSHER SALT, PLUS MORE TO TASTE

2 TABLESPOONS BLACK PEPPER

2 TABLESPOONS APPLE CIDER VINEGAR

1½ CUPS CHICKEN STOCK (SEE PAGE 30 FOR HOMEMADE)

2 STAR ANISE PODS

3 BAY LEAVES

DIRECTIONS

1. Place all of the ingredients in a slow cooker, making sure the pork shoulder rests on top of the vegetables. Cover and cook on low until the pork is very tender, about 5 to 6 hours.

2. Remove the cinnamon stick, star anise pods, and bay leaves. Ladle the vegetables and some of the juice into a bowl. Remove the pork shoulder and shred into large pieces with a fork. To serve, place pieces of the pork shoulder on top of the vegetables and ladle the juices over the top.

Shengjian Baozi

YIELD: **4 SERVINGS**

ACTIVE TIME: **1 HOUR**

TOTAL TIME: **2 HOURS**

The origin of the steamed pork buns that have won the hearts of foodies all over America.

INGREDIENTS

FOR THE WRAPPERS

1 TABLESPOON INSTANT YEAST

1½ CUPS WATER, AT ROOM TEMPERATURE

¼ CUP VEGETABLE OIL, PLUS MORE AS NEEDED

¼ CUP SUGAR, PLUS 1 TEASPOON

½ TEASPOON KOSHER SALT

4 TEASPOONS BAKING POWDER

2 CUPS ALL-PURPOSE FLOUR, PLUS MORE FOR DUSTING.

2 CUPS BREAD FLOUR

FOR THE FILLING

10 OZ. GROUND PORK

1 TABLESPOON PEELED AND MINCED GINGER

⅓ CUP CHOPPED SCALLIONS

¼ TEASPOON KOSHER SALT

PINCH OF WHITE PEPPER

Continued...

DIRECTIONS

---

1. To prepare the wrappers, place the yeast, water, and oil in a small bowl and let stand until foamy, about 10 minutes. Place the sugar, salt, baking powder, and flours in a food processor and pulse for 15 seconds to combine. With the food processor running on low speed, add the yeast mixture and keep it running until it comes together as a slightly tacky dough. Place the dough on a flour-dusted work surface and knead until it is smooth, about 3 minutes. Place the dough in a bowl greased with vegetable oil, cover with a kitchen towel, and let rise in a naturally warm place until it has doubled in size, about 30 minutes. Place the dough on the flour-dusted work surface, cut it in half, and roll each half into a log. Cut each log into eight pieces. Roll each piece into a 4" circle and cover with a kitchen towel so that they do not dry out.

2. To prepare the filling, place the pork, ginger, and scallions in a mixing bowl and stir to combine. Place the remaining ingredients, except for the vegetable oil, in a separate bowl and stir until the salt and sugar have dissolved. Pour the liquid mixture over the pork mixture and stir to incorporate. Cover the mixing bowl and let sit for 30 minutes.

3. Place a wrapper in the palm of one hand and add about 1 tablespoon of the pork mixture. Cup the wrapper and close it over the filling. Squeeze it so that it is tightly sealed and twist to remove any excess dough. Place the filled dumplings, seam-side down, on a parchment-lined baking sheet and let them rise until doubled in size, about 30 minutes.

Continued...

1 TEASPOON SUGAR

1 TABLESPOON SOY SAUCE, PLUS 1 TEASPOON

2 TEASPOONS RICE WINE VINEGAR

2 TEASPOONS SESAME OIL

1 TABLESPOON HOT WATER (125°F), PLUS MORE AS NEEDED

¼ CUP VEGETABLE OIL

4. Warm half of the vegetable oil in a skillet over medium heat. Working in two batches, arrange the buns so that they are at least ½" apart. Cook until golden brown on both sides, about 2 minutes per side. Add hot water until it is ¼" deep, and hold the cover of the pan in front of you to prevent being harmed by any oil splattering. Cover the pan and cook until the water has evaporated, about 6 minutes. Remove the lid and cook until the bottom is crispy, about 2 minutes. Transfer the cooked baozi to a plate, tent the plate with aluminum foil to keep them warm, and repeat the cooking process with the remaining baozi. When all of the baozi have been cooked, serve immediately.

INGREDIENTS

2 CUPS FARRO

3 EARS OF CORN, HUSKED AND RINSED

4-LB., SKIN-ON PORK BELLY

1 TABLESPOON KOSHER SALT, PLUS MORE TO TASTE

BLACK PEPPER, TO TASTE

2 TABLESPOONS OLIVE OIL

2 LARGE YELLOW ONIONS, CUT INTO 1" PIECES

2 LARGE CARROTS, CUT INTO 1" PIECES

4 CELERY STALKS, CUT INTO 1" PIECES

6 GARLIC CLOVES, CRUSHED

6 SPRIGS OF THYME

3 TABLESPOONS TOMATO PASTE

2 CUPS WHITE WINE

8 CUPS CHICKEN STOCK (SEE PAGE 30 FOR HOMEMADE)

6 CUPS WATER

1 SHALLOT, HALVED

1 BAY LEAF

4 OZ. SNAP PEAS, TRIMMED AND CHOPPED

4 TABLESPOONS UNSALTED BUTTER

¼ CUP SLICED CHIVES

Braised Pork Belly with Toasted Farro, Corn & Snap Peas

Whenever you mention pork belly, you get a group of people saying "I don't like it … there's too much fat." While it is true that the belly does have a high-fat content, it will render off if cooked properly, resulting in a delicious, tender piece of meat.

DIRECTIONS

1. The night before you are going to serve the preparation, preheat the oven to 350°F and place the farro on a rimmed baking sheet in an even layer. Place it in the oven and bake until the farro is a deep brown. Remove from the oven, place it in a bowl, factoring in that the grains will double in size, and cover with the water. Soak overnight.

2. Preheat the oven to 350°F. Place the ears of corn in the oven and cook until the kernels give slightly when squeezed. Remove from the oven and let cool. Lower the oven temperature to 250°F.

3. Place the pork belly skin-side down on a surface and use a knife to score the flesh, slicing ¼" deep in a crosshatch pattern. Season with salt and pepper and set aside.

4. Place the olive oil in a large Dutch oven and warm over high heat. When the oil starts to shimmer, carefully place the pork belly, skin-side down, in the pot to begin rendering the fat. Sear until the skin is brown, turn over, and sear until brown on the other side. Remove the pork belly from the pot and set aside.

Continued…

5. Add the onions, carrots, celery, and garlic to the Dutch oven and cook, stirring frequently, until the onion starts to brown, about 6 minutes. Add 4 sprigs of thyme and the tomato paste, stir to coat the vegetables, and then add the wine. Scrape up any browned bits from the bottom of the Dutch oven and cook until the liquid starts to thicken. Add the stock, bring to a boil, and return the pork belly to the pot. Cover the Dutch oven and transfer it to the oven. Cook until the pork belly is very tender, 2 to 2½ hours.

6. When the pork belly is tender, strain and reserve the liquid, discard the vegetables, set the pork belly aside, and place the liquid in a saucepan. Cook over high heat until it is thick and syrupy. Set aside.

7. Drain the farro and place it in a large pot with the water, shallot, 1 tablespoon salt, remaining thyme, and bay leaf. Bring to a boil over medium-high heat and then reduce the heat so that the mixture simmers. Cook until the farro is al dente, about 20 minutes. Remove the shallot, thyme, and bay leaf, drain, and transfer to a bowl.

8. Remove the kernels from the roasted ears of corn. Bring a small pot of salted water to boil, add the snap peas, and cook for 1 minute. Drain and add to the farro along with the corn, butter, and chives. Stir to combine, season with salt and pepper, and transfer to a serving dish.

9. Slice the pork belly and place the slices on top of the farro-and-corn mixture. Spoon the reduced cooking liquid over the top and serve.

Pork with Blue Cheese Polenta & Roasted Peach Hot Sauce

Just because a peach is overly ripe doesn't mean that it's no good, as this sweet, sour, and spicy sauce proves.

YIELD: **6 TO 8 SERVINGS**

ACTIVE TIME: **40 MINUTES**

TOTAL TIME: **6 HOURS**

INGREDIENTS

6- TO 8-LB., BONE-IN PORK SHOULDER

SALT AND PEPPER, TO TASTE

1 LARGE YELLOW ONION, DICED

3 BAY LEAVES

2 TEASPOONS PAPRIKA

¼ CUP BROWN SUGAR

2 TABLESPOONS PEPPERCORNS

7 CUPS CHICKEN STOCK (SEE PAGE 30 FOR HOMEMADE)

1 TABLESPOON MUSTARD

2 CUPS CORNMEAL

2 CUPS WATER

1 STICK UNSALTED BUTTER

1 CUP CRUMBLED BLUE CHEESE

8 OVERLY RIPE PEACHES, PITTED AND QUARTERED

2 CUPS APPLE CIDER VINEGAR

Continued…

DIRECTIONS

1. Preheat the oven to 300°F. Season the pork generously with salt.

2. Place the pork shoulder in a large skillet and cook, while turning, over medium-high heat until browned on each side.

3. Transfer the pork shoulder to a Dutch oven and add the onion, bay leaves, paprika, brown sugar, peppercorns, 4 cups of the stock, and mustard.

4. Cover the Dutch oven and place in the oven until the pork is fork-tender, about 4 hours. Remove from the oven, let cool slightly, and then shred with a fork.

5. Approximately 1 hour before the pulled pork will be finished cooking, place the cornmeal, the remaining 3 cups of stock, and the water in a large pot. Bring to a boil over medium-high heat, reduce heat so that the mixture simmers, and cook, while stirring frequently, until the mixture is thick, about 40 minutes to 1 hour.

6. Add half of the butter and stir to combine. Stir half of the blue cheese into the pot, season with salt and pepper, and remove from heat. Set aside.

7. Once you have removed the pork shoulder from the oven, raise the oven temperature to 400°F.

Continued…

¾ CUP SUGAR

3 GARLIC CLOVES, CHOPPED

6 JALAPEÑO PEPPERS, STEMMED, SEEDED, AND DICED

4 CAYENNE PEPPERS, STEMMED, SEEDED, AND DICED

8. Place the peaches skin-side down on a baking sheet and place them in the oven. Cook until they began to darken, about 10 minutes. You can also grill the peaches if you're after a slightly smokier sauce.

9. Remove the peaches from the oven and place in a medium saucepan. Add the vinegar, sugar, garlic, peppers and bring to a simmer over medium-low heat. Simmer for 10 minutes, transfer the mixture to a blender, and puree until smooth. Set the hot sauce aside.

10. Stir the remaining butter into the polenta and then spoon the polenta into warmed bowls. Lay some of the pulled pork over it, and top with the hot sauce and remaining blue cheese.

Fettuccine in Spicy Pork Sauce

YIELD: **6 TO 8 SERVINGS**

ACTIVE TIME: **30 MINUTES**

TOTAL TIME: **2 HOURS**

This aromatic sauce is a perfect illustration of how effective low and slow cooking can be.

INGREDIENTS

6 TABLESPOONS UNSALTED BUTTER

1 YELLOW ONION, GRATED

2 CELERY STALKS, GRATED

SALT, TO TASTE

1½ LBS. GROUND PORK

1 CUP WHOLE MILK

5 WHOLE CLOVES

1 CUP CHICKEN STOCK (SEE PAGE 30 FOR HOMEMADE)

2 TABLESPOONS TOMATO PASTE

2 BAY LEAVES

RED PEPPER FLAKES, TO TASTE

1 LB. FETTUCCINE

DIRECTIONS

1. Place the butter in a Dutch oven and melt over medium-high heat. Add the onion and celery, season with salt, and stir to combine. When the vegetables start to sizzle, reduce the heat to low, cover, and cook, stirring occasionally, until the vegetables are very tender, about 30 minutes.

2. Add the ground pork, raise the heat to medium-high, and cook, while using a wooden spoon to break up the meat, until the pork starts to brown, about 6 minutes. Add the milk and cook until it has evaporated, about 10 minutes. Add the cloves, cook for 2 minutes, and then add the stock, tomato paste, bay leaves, and red pepper flakes. Bring to a boil, reduce the heat to low, cover, and simmer for 45 minutes, while stirring occasionally. You'll know the sauce is ready when the fat has separated and is bubbling on the surface.

3. While the sauce is simmering, bring a large pot of salted water to a boil. Add the fettuccine and briefly stir to prevent sticking. Cook until al dente, 6 to 8 minutes, and then drain. Add to the sauce and toss to combine or serve the sauce on the side.

Chipotle Sausage & Peppers

YIELD: **6 SERVINGS**

ACTIVE TIME: **15 MINUTES**

TOTAL TIME: **4 HOURS**

The smoky bite of the chipotle peppers puts a new twist on a ballpark favorite.

INGREDIENTS

5 BELL PEPPERS, STEMMED, SEEDED, AND SLICED

1 (28 OZ.) CAN OF FIRE-ROASTED TOMATOES

3 GARLIC CLOVES

2 CHIPOTLE PEPPERS EN ADOBO

1 TABLESPOON ADOBO SAUCE

2 LBS. KIELBASA, CUT INTO 6 EVEN PIECES

1 HABANERO PEPPER, PIERCED

SUBMARINE ROLLS, FOR SERVING (OPTIONAL)

DIRECTIONS

1. Place the bell peppers in a slow cooker and set it to high heat. Place the tomatoes, garlic, chipotle peppers, and adobo sauce in a blender and puree until smooth. Pour the puree over the peppers and stir to combine.

2. Add the kielbasa and the habanero to the slow cooker, cover, and cook on high for 4 hours.

3. Discard the habanero. Ladle into warmed bowls or submarine rolls and serve immediately.

Porchetta

YIELD: **12 SERVINGS**

ACTIVE TIME: **30 MINUTES**

TOTAL TIME: **2 DAYS**

If you've never had this crispy, tender, rich wonder, be prepared to fall madly in love.

INGREDIENTS

5- TO 6-LB., SKIN-ON PORK BELLY

1 TABLESPOON FRESH ROSEMARY LEAVES, MINCED

1 TABLESPOON FRESH THYME LEAVES, MINCED

1 TABLESPOON MINCED FRESH SAGE LEAVES

2 TEASPOONS GARLIC POWDER

SALT, TO TASTE

1-LB. CENTER-CUT PORK TENDERLOIN

DIRECTIONS

1. Place the pork belly skin-side down on a cutting board. Using a sharp knife, score the flesh in a crosshatch pattern. Flip the pork belly over and poke small holes in the skin. Turn the pork belly back over and rub the minced herbs, garlic powder, and salt into the flesh. Place the pork tenderloin in the center of the pork belly and then roll the pork belly so that it retains its length. Tie the rolled-up pork belly securely with kitchen twine every ½".

2. Transfer the pork belly to a rack with a large pan underneath, place it in the fridge, and leave uncovered for 2 days. This allows the skin to dry out a bit. Pat the pork belly occasionally with paper towels to remove excess moisture.

3. Remove the pork belly from the refrigerator and let stand at room temperature for 1 to 2 hours. Preheat the oven to 480°F. When the pork belly is room temperature, place the rack and the pan in the oven and cook for 35 minutes, turning the pork belly occasionally to ensure even cooking.

4. Reduce the oven temperature to 300°F and cook until a meat thermometer inserted into the center reaches 145°F, about 1 to 2 hours. The porchetta's skin should be crispy. If it is not as crispy as you'd like, raise the oven's temperature to 500°F and cook until crispy. Remove from the oven and let the porchetta rest for 15 minutes before slicing.

Bulgogi with Musaengchae

YIELD: **4 SERVINGS**

ACTIVE TIME: **5 MINUTES**

TOTAL TIME: **45 MINUTES**

In Korean, **bul** *means "fire" and* **gogi** *translates to "meat." When you come across a dish that trumpets such simplicity, you can be sure you've got a winner. You can find* **gochujang** *online or in well-stocked grocery stores, and the subtle heat it adds makes it worth tracking down.*

INGREDIENTS

2 LBS. PORK TENDERLOIN, SLICED THIN

4 GARLIC CLOVES, MINCED

1 TABLESPOON MINCED GINGER

½ CUP GOCHUJANG (KOREAN CHILI PASTE)

2 TABLESPOONS SOY SAUCE

3 TABLESPOONS SESAME OIL

SESAME SEEDS, FOR GARNISH

2 SCALLIONS, CHOPPED, FOR GARNISH

MUSAENGCHAE (SEE SIDEBAR), FOR SERVING

DIRECTIONS

1. Place all of the ingredients, except for the garnishes and Musaengchae, in a bowl and stir to combine. Let the meat marinate for at least 30 minutes and up to an hour.

2. Warm a 12" cast-iron skillet over high heat for 5 minutes. When it is extremely hot, add the marinated pork and sear, turning the pork as it browns, until it is cooked through, about 5 minutes.

3. Garnish with the sesame seeds and chopped scallions and serve with the Musaengchae.

MUSAENGCHAE

3 cups shredded daikon radish

1 teaspoon Korean chili powder

2 tablespoons rice vinegar

1 tablespoon kosher salt

1 tablespoon sugar

1. Place all of the ingredients in a mixing bowl and stir to combine.

2. Let stand for at least 1 hour before serving.

CHAPTER 4

LAMB

Many people shy away from lamb, but we're betting that wariness has more to do with a failure of execution, and not a shortcoming of the ingredient. It is flavorful and delicate, and so versatile that it can shine whether freighted with an herbal, sweet, smoky, or spicy accent. But it is also easy to overcook, and frequently partnered with an uninspired, viscous mint sauce.

The preparations in this chapter are out to convert those whose experience of lamb has thus far been lacking. From the subtle heat of the Spicy Lamb Chops with Raita (see page 116) and sweetness of the Braised Lamb with Minty Peas (see page 120) to the effortless decadence of the Roasted Rack of Lamb with Garlic & Herb Crust (see page 124), we're sure that even the strongest skeptics will find something that softens their stance.

Spicy Lamb Chops with Raita

YIELD: **4 SERVINGS**

ACTIVE TIME: **15 MINUTES**

TOTAL TIME: **1 HOUR AND 30 MINUTES**

The refreshing tang of raita tempers the smoky heat cooked into these lamb chops.

INGREDIENTS

FOR THE LAMB

3 TABLESPOONS CHILI POWDER

3 TABLESPOONS SMOKED PAPRIKA

1 TABLESPOON DRIED OREGANO

2 TEASPOONS CUMIN

2 TEASPOONS BLACK PEPPER

2 TEASPOONS KOSHER SALT

1 TEASPOON DRIED THYME

4 LAMB CHOPS (EACH 1" THICK)

FOR THE RAITA

1 CUP PLAIN YOGURT

2 TEASPOONS MINCED RED ONION

½ CUP SEEDED AND CHOPPED PERSIAN CUCUMBER

2 TABLESPOONS MINCED FRESH CILANTRO

FOR SERVING

LEMON WEDGES

DIRECTIONS

1. To begin preparations for the lamb, place the seasonings in a small bowl and stir to combine. Generously apply the mixture to both sides of the lamb chops and let stand at room temperature for 1 hour.

2. To prepare the raita, place all of the ingredients in a mixing bowl and stir to combine. Cover and store in the refrigerator.

3. Preheat your gas or charcoal grill to medium-high heat.

4. When the grill is at 450°F, place the lamb chops on the grill and cook for 3 minutes. Turn the chops over and cook for another 3 minutes for medium-rare, and 4 minutes for medium. The lamb chops should feel slightly firm in the center. Transfer the chops to a cutting board and let rest for 10 minutes before serving with the raita and lemon wedges.

Lamb Kebabs with Succotash

YIELD: **4 SERVINGS**

ACTIVE TIME: **30 MINUTES**

TOTAL TIME: **4 HOURS AND 30 MINUTES**

A long bath in wine and garlic makes for sweet, tender kebabs.

INGREDIENTS

FOR THE LAMB KEBABS

2 LBS. BONELESS LEG OF LAMB, CUT INTO 1½" CUBES

SALT AND PEPPER, TO TASTE

3 TABLESPOONS OLIVE OIL

1½ CUPS RED WINE

4 GARLIC CLOVES, CRUSHED

1 SHALLOT, MINCED

2 TEASPOONS MINCED ROSEMARY

1 TEASPOON GROUND CUMIN

24 SKEWERS

2 RED ONIONS, CHOPPED

2 RED BELL PEPPERS, CHOPPED

FOR THE SUCCOTASH

1 CUP SLICED MUSHROOM CAPS

1 RED ONION, MINCED

4 CUPS CORN KERNELS

1 RED BELL PEPPER, STEMMED, SEEDED, AND DICED

2 CUPS FRESH OR FROZEN EDAMAME

1 TABLESPOON UNSALTED BUTTER

SALT AND PEPPER, TO TASTE

1 TABLESPOON MINCED FRESH MARJORAM

½ CUP CHOPPED FRESH BASIL

DIRECTIONS

1. To begin preparations for the lamb kebabs, place all of the ingredients, except for the skewers, onions, and peppers, in a large resealable plastic bag. Toss to combine, place the bag in the refrigerator, and marinate for 4 hours. If time allows, marinate the lamb overnight.

2. Remove the bag from the refrigerator about 1 hour before you are going to start grilling. Transfer the lamb to a platter and let rest at room temperature.

3. To prepare the succotash, place a large cast-iron skillet over medium heat, add the mushrooms and cook until they release their liquid and start to brown, about 8 minutes. Reduce heat to low and cook until the mushrooms are a deep brown, about 15 minutes. Place the onion in the skillet, raise heat to medium-high, and cook until it has softened, about 5 minutes. Add the corn, bell pepper, and edamame and cook, while stirring often, until the corn is tender and bright yellow, about 4 minutes. Add the butter and stir until it has melted and coated all of the vegetables. Season with salt and pepper, add the marjoram and basil, stir to incorporate, and set aside.

4. Preheat your gas or charcoal grill to medium-high heat and assemble the skewers. Place approximately 4 pieces of lamb on each skewer, making sure to align the pieces of onion and pepper in between each piece of lamb.

5. Once the grill is about 450°F, place the skewers on the grill and cook, while turning, until the lamb is medium-rare and browned all over, about 10 to 12 minutes. Transfer the kebabs to a large cutting board and let them rest for 5 minutes before serving with the succotash.

Braised Lamb with Minty Peas

YIELD: **4 TO 6 SERVINGS**

ACTIVE TIME: **30 MINUTES**

TOTAL TIME: **1 HOUR AND 30 MINUTES**

Don't hesitate to break this out for company, as it is delicious and the honey helps squash the gamy quality that makes some people lukewarm about lamb.

INGREDIENTS

FOR THE LAMB

2 TABLESPOONS OLIVE OIL

1 YELLOW ONION, CHOPPED

2 LBS. BONELESS LAMB SHOULDER, CUT INTO 1" CHUNKS

SALT AND PEPPER, TO TASTE

½ CUP HONEY

1 GARLIC CLOVE, MINCED

1 TEASPOON CORIANDER

½ TEASPOON CUMIN (OPTIONAL)

¼ TEASPOON CAYENNE PEPPER, OR TO TASTE

1 TEASPOON GROUND CARAWAY

½ TEASPOON GROUND FENNEL

1 CUP CHICKEN OR BEEF STOCK (SEE PAGE 30 OR PAGE 67, RESPECTIVELY, FOR HOMEMADE)

1 CUP SLIVERED ALMONDS

FRESH LEMON JUICE, TO TASTE

FOR THE PEAS

3 SPRIGS OF MINT

3 CUPS PEAS

DIRECTIONS

1. To begin preparations for the lamb, place the oil in a large, deep skillet and warm over medium heat. When the oil starts to shimmer, add the onion and cook until soft, about 10 minutes. Remove with a slotted spoon and raise heat to medium-high. Add the lamb, season with salt and pepper, and cook, turning frequently, until the pieces are browned all over.

2. Turn off heat and let the pan cool slightly. Turn heat back to medium and add the honey. Cook, stirring, until honey has thinned and the lamb is coated. Stir in the garlic, add the seasonings and stock, and return the onions to the pan. Cover the pan and simmer until the meat is very tender, about 1 hour.

3. Prepare the peas when the lamb is close to done. Place the sprigs of mint and peas in a saucepan and cover with water. Cook over medium heat until the peas are tender, approximately 4 minutes for fresh peas and 7 minutes if using frozen. Drain, discard the mint, and cover the pan to keep warm.

4. Taste the lamb and adjust the seasoning as necessary. Stir in the almonds, stir in the lemon juice, and serve with the peas.

Grilled Lamb Loin with Quinoa & Radish Leaf Chimichurri

YIELD: **6 SERVINGS**

ACTIVE TIME: **45 MINUTES**

TOTAL TIME: **3 HOURS AND 30 MINUTES**

Utilizing radish leaves in the chimichurri achieves the expected flavor and helps cut down on food waste.

INGREDIENTS

FOR THE LAMB & QUINOA

2½-LB. LAMB LOIN

LAMB MARINADE (SEE SIDEBAR)

2 CUPS QUINOA

4½ CUPS WATER

1 SMALL SHALLOT, TRIMMED AND HALVED

2 TEASPOONS KOSHER SALT, PLUS MORE TO TASTE

6 BABY BOK CHOY, TRIMMED

10 RADISHES, TRIMMED AND QUARTERED, TOPS RESERVED

BLACK PEPPER, TO TASTE

2 TABLESPOONS FRESH LEMON JUICE

FOR THE CHIMICHURRI

1 SMALL SHALLOT, MINCED

2 GARLIC CLOVES, MINCED

¼ TEASPOON RED PEPPER FLAKES

Continued...

DIRECTIONS

1. To begin preparations for the lamb and quinoa, trim the fat from the lamb loin. Rub with the marinade and let it marinate in the refrigerator for at least 2 hours. Remove approximately 45 minutes prior to grilling.

2. Place the quinoa in a fine sieve and run under cold water until the water is clear. Place the quinoa in a medium saucepan and cover with the water. Add the shallot and salt and bring to a boil. Cover the pan and lower the temperature so that the quinoa simmers. Cook until all the liquid has been absorbed, about 20 minutes. Remove the shallot, spread the quinoa in an even layer on a parchment-lined baking sheet, and let cool.

3. Bring a pot of salted water to a boil and prepare an ice water bath. Rinse the bok choy under cold water and place in the boiling water. Cook for 1 minute, remove with a strainer, and transfer to the ice water bath.

4. Let the water come back to a boil and then add the radish tops. Cook for 1 minute, remove with a strainer, and transfer to the ice water bath. When the vegetables have cooled completely, drain, pat dry, and place in a mixing bowl. Season with salt and pepper, add the quartered radishes and lemon juice, and toss to evenly coat. Set aside.

Continued...

¼ CUP RED WINE VINEGAR

⅔ CUP CHOPPED RADISH LEAVES

1 TABLESPOON MINCED OREGANO

½ CUP OLIVE OIL

2 TEASPOONS KOSHER SALT, PLUS
MORE TO TASTE

5. Preheat your gas or charcoal grill to medium-high heat. When the grill is about 450°F, place the lamb on the grill and cook, while turning, until the loin is seared on all sides and the internal temperature is 140°F. Remove from the grill and let sit for 10 minutes before slicing.

6. To prepare the chimichurri, place all of the ingredients in a mixing bowl and whisk until combined. Season to taste and set aside.

7. To serve, place the quinoa and vegetables on a plate and top with slices of the lamb. Drizzle the chimichurri over the top or serve it on the side.

LAMB MARINADE

8 garlic cloves, minced

1 tablespoon cumin

2 tablespoons black pepper

1 tablespoon ground fennel

1 tablespoon paprika

2 tablespoons kosher salt

2 teaspoons Dijon mustard

1 cup olive oil

1. Place all of the ingredients in a mixing bowl and stir until combined.

Roasted Rack of Lamb with Garlic & Herb Crust

YIELD: **4 TO 6 SERVINGS**

ACTIVE TIME: **20 MINUTES**

TOTAL TIME: **24 HOURS**

Marinating the rack of lamb overnight allows for the quick cooking this very delicate cut of meat requires.

INGREDIENTS

FOR THE LAMB

2 TABLESPOONS OLIVE OIL

2 GARLIC CLOVES, MINCED

1 TEASPOON LEMON ZEST

2 (8-RIB) RACKS OF LAMB

SALT AND PEPPER, TO TASTE

FOR THE GARLIC & HERB CRUST

4 GARLIC CLOVES, MINCED

½ SMALL SHALLOT, MINCED

¼ CUP CHOPPED FRESH PARSLEY

2 TABLESPOONS FRESH ROSEMARY LEAVES, MINCED

1 TABLESPOON FRESH THYME LEAVES, MINCED

1 TABLESPOON OLIVE OIL

SALT AND PEPPER, TO TASTE

DIRECTIONS

1. To begin preparations for the lamb, place the olive oil, garlic, and lemon zest in a large resealable plastic bag. Pat the racks of lamb dry, season with salt and pepper, and use your hands to work the seasonings into the lamb. Place the racks of lamb in the plastic bag, place it in the refrigerator, and marinate overnight.

2. Remove the racks of lamb from the refrigerator about 1 hour before you are going to start grilling. Remove from the bag and let them come to room temperature.

3. Preheat your gas or charcoal grill to medium heat and prepare the crust. Place all of the ingredients in a small bowl and stir to combine. Generously apply the mixture to the lamb, being sure to apply the majority on the meaty side of the racks.

4. When the grill is about 400°F, place the meaty side of the racks of lamb on the grill and cook for about 3 to 4 minutes. When the crusts are browned, flip the racks of lamb over and grill for another 5 minutes for medium-rare.

5. Transfer the racks of lamb from the grill to a large cutting board and let rest for about 10 minutes before slicing and serving.

Lamb & Sweet Potato Hash

YIELD: **4 TO 6 SERVINGS**

ACTIVE TIME: **20 MINUTES**

TOTAL TIME: **24 HOURS**

If you really want to take this dish to the next level, place a fried egg on top of each portion.

INGREDIENTS

FOR THE MARINADE

4 GARLIC CLOVES, MASHED

LEAVES FROM 3 SPRIGS OREGANO

¼ CUP DIJON MUSTARD

¼ CUP CABERNET SAUVIGNON

1 TABLESPOON KOSHER SALT

1 TABLESPOON BLACK PEPPER

FOR THE LAMB & SWEET POTATO HASH

1½-LB. LEG OF LAMB, BUTTERFLIED

4 TABLESPOONS CLARIFIED UNSALTED BUTTER

2 CUPS WATER

1 LB. SWEET POTATOES, PEELED AND MINCED

2 POBLANO PEPPERS, STEMMED, SEEDED, AND DICED

2 YELLOW ONIONS, MINCED

2 GARLIC CLOVES, MINCED

1 TABLESPOON CUMIN

1 TABLESPOON KOSHER SALT, PLUS MORE TO TASTE

1 TABLESPOON CHOPPED FRESH OREGANO

BLACK PEPPER, TO TASTE

DIRECTIONS

1. To prepare the marinade, place all of the ingredients in a small bowl, stir to combine, and then transfer the mixture to a resealable plastic bag. To begin preparations for the lamb and hash, place the lamb in the bag, place in the refrigerator, and marinate overnight.

2. Preheat the oven to 350°F. Place a cast-iron skillet over medium-high heat and add half of the clarified butter. Remove the lamb from the bag, place it in the skillet, and sear for 5 minutes on each side.

3. Add the water to the skillet, place it in the oven, and cook for 20 minutes, or until the center of the lamb reaches 140°F. Remove the skillet from the oven, transfer the lamb to a cutting board or platter, and drain the liquid from the skillet. Let the lamb sit for 15 minutes and then mince.

4. Fill the skillet with water and bring to a boil. Add the sweet potatoes and cook until they are just tender, about 7 minutes. Be careful not to overcook them, as you don't want to end up with mashed potatoes. Drain the potatoes and set aside.

5. Add the remaining clarified butter, the poblano peppers, onions, garlic, and cumin to the skillet and cook over medium heat until all of the vegetables are soft, about 10 minutes.

6. Return the potatoes and the lamb to the skillet. Add the salt and cook for another 15 minutes. Add the oregano, stir to incorporate, season with salt and pepper, and serve.

Leg of Lamb with Rosemary & Mustard Marinade

YIELD: **4 SERVINGS**

ACTIVE TIME: **30 MINUTES**

TOTAL TIME: **1 HOUR**

The rosemary and mustard make fast friends with a leg of lamb, but a bit of char from the grill takes the relationship to the next level.

INGREDIENTS

3 TABLESPOONS OLIVE OIL

¼ CUP ROSEMARY LEAVES, MINCED

¼ CUP DIJON MUSTARD

4 GARLIC CLOVES, MINCED

1 LARGE SHALLOT, MINCED

1½ TEASPOONS FRESH LEMON JUICE

1 TABLESPOON MINCED FRESH PARSLEY, PLUS MORE FOR GARNISH

SALT AND PEPPER, TO TASTE

6-LB. LEG OF LAMB, BUTTERFLIED AND BONED

LEMON WEDGES, FOR SERVING

DIRECTIONS

1. Place all of the ingredients, except for the leg of lamb and lemon wedges, in a small bowl and stir to combine. Place ¼ cup of the marinade in a small airtight container and cover it.

2. Place the leg of lamb on a rack in a roasting pan. Massage the remaining marinade into the leg of lamb. Cover the leg of lamb with aluminum foil and let stand at room temperature for 2 hours.

3. Preheat your gas or charcoal grill to medium-high heat. When the grill is about 450°F, place the marinated leg of lamb on the grill and cook for about 16 minutes per side for medium-rare, 18 minutes for medium. While grilling, brush the reserved marinade on top of the lamb. Transfer the lamb to a large cutting board and let rest for 15 minutes.

4. Slice the lamb into ½" wide strips, garnish with additional parsley, and serve with lemon wedges.

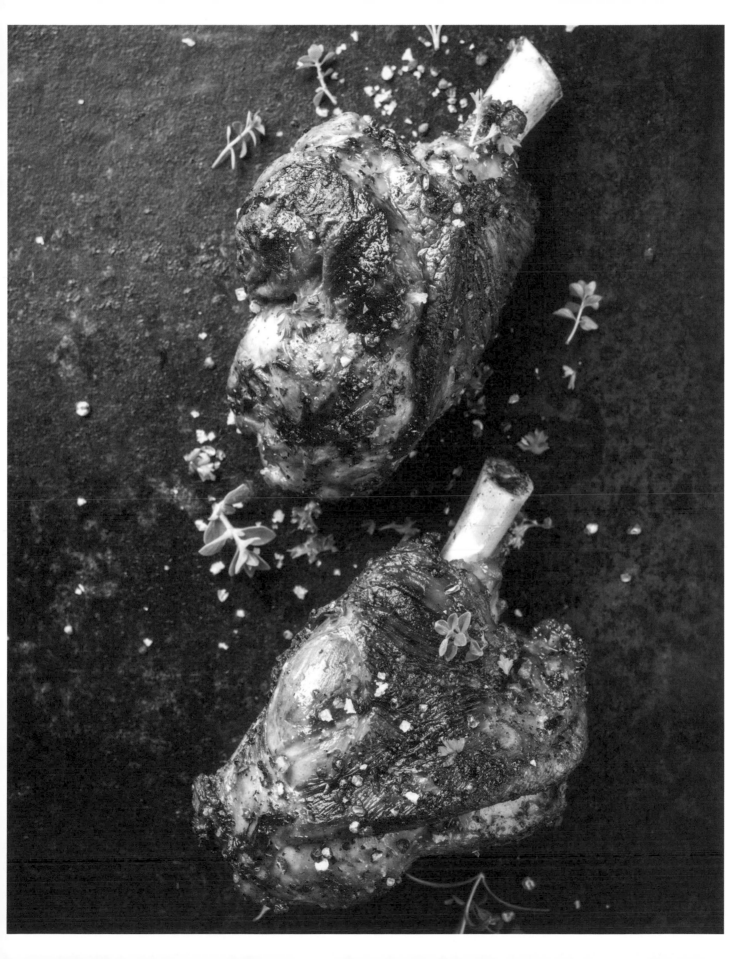

Rogan Josh

YIELD: **4 SERVINGS**

ACTIVE TIME: **20 MINUTES**

TOTAL TIME: **1 HOUR AND 30 MINUTES**

Pressed for time? This can also be a fantastic make-ahead dish that tastes just as good—if not better—the next day.

INGREDIENTS

¼ CUP OLIVE OIL

2 LBS. BONELESS LAMB SHOULDER, CUT INTO 1" PIECES

SALT, TO TASTE

2 LARGE YELLOW ONIONS, SLICED THIN

2 TABLESPOONS MINCED GINGER

2 GARLIC CLOVES, MINCED

1 TABLESPOON CURRY POWDER, PLUS 1 TEASPOON

1 TEASPOON TURMERIC

1 TEASPOON CAYENNE PEPPER, OR TO TASTE

1 TEASPOON GARAM MASALA

1 (14 OZ.) CAN OF CRUSHED TOMATOES

1 CUP PLAIN YOGURT

2 CUPS WATER

FRESH CILANTRO, CHOPPED, FOR GARNISH

RED ONION, DICED, FOR GARNISH

DIRECTIONS

1. Place the oil in a Dutch oven and warm over high heat. Season the lamb with salt. When the oil starts to shimmer, add the lamb and cook, while turning occasionally, until it is lightly browned all over, about 12 minutes. Remove with a slotted spoon and set aside.

2. Add the yellow onions, ginger, garlic, curry, turmeric, cayenne, and garam masala to the Dutch oven and sauté for 2 minutes. Add the tomatoes, yogurt, and water and bring to a gentle boil. Return the lamb to the pot, lower the heat, cover, and simmer until the lamb is very tender, about 1 hour. Remove the cover occasionally to stir and make sure the rogan josh does not burn.

3. Ladle into warmed bowls and garnish with the cilantro and red onion.

Curry Burgers

YIELD: **4 SERVINGS**

ACTIVE TIME: **15 MINUTES**

TOTAL TIME: **40 MINUTES**

Switch up your burger game with this spicy, Indian-influenced twist and you've got a signature dish for a backyard barbecue. If it's more of a casual affair than a sit-down dinner, you can also form the mixture into meatballs and serve as an appetizer.

INGREDIENTS

1 LB. GROUND LAMB

½ LB. GROUND BEEF

2 TABLESPOONS CURRY POWDER

1 TEASPOON CAYENNE PEPPER, OR TO TASTE

½ TEASPOON MUSTARD POWDER

½ RED ONION, MINCED

2 TEASPOONS MINCED GINGER

3 GARLIC CLOVES, MINCED

½ CUP CHOPPED FRESH CILANTRO, PLUS MORE FOR SERVING

1 LARGE EGG

SALT AND PEPPER, TO TASTE

4 WHOLE-WHEAT HAMBURGER BUNS, FOR SERVING

TOMATO CHUTNEY (SEE SIDEBAR), FOR SERVING

DIRECTIONS

1. Place all of the ingredients, except for those designated for serving, in a large bowl and stir gently until just combined. Divide into 4 thick patties and let rest for 20 minutes at room temperature.

2. Preheat your grill to medium-high heat or warm a cast-iron skillet over medium-high heat. When the grill is 450°F or the skillet is hot, add the burgers and cook until cooked through, about 6 minutes per side. Remove from heat and let rest for 5 minutes.

3. Serve on the hamburger buns alongside the additional cilantro and Tomato Chutney.

TOMATO CHUTNEY

1 tablespoon olive oil

½ cup minced onion

½ teaspoon curry powder

½ teaspoon cumin

½ teaspoon grated ginger

2 large red tomatoes, seeded and diced

½ cup apple cider vinegar

¼ cup sugar

½ teaspoon kosher salt

1. Place the oil in a saucepan and warm over medium-high heat. When the oil starts to shimmer, add the onion and sauté until translucent, about 3 minutes. Add the curry powder, cumin, and ginger and cook for another 2 minutes.

2. Add the tomatoes, vinegar, sugar, and salt, raise the heat to high, and bring to a boil. Reduce the heat and let the mixture simmer until it has reduced by about two-thirds, about 15 minutes.

3. Transfer the mixture to a food processor and pulse until it is blended but still slightly chunky. Store in an airtight container in the refrigerator for up to 2 weeks.

Kefta with Chickpea Salad

YIELD: **4 TO 6 SERVINGS**

ACTIVE TIME: **35 MINUTES**

TOTAL TIME: **24 HOURS**

Think of kefta as a Moroccan meatball where the lemon zest lends a welcome brightness to these typically earthy elements.

INGREDIENTS

FOR THE KEFTA

1½ LBS. GROUND LAMB

½ LB. GROUND BEEF

½ CUP MINCED WHITE ONION

2 GARLIC CLOVES, ROASTED AND MASHED

ZEST OF 1 LEMON

1 CUP PARSLEY, WASHED AND MINCED

2 TABLESPOONS CHOPPED MINT

1 TEASPOON CINNAMON

2 TABLESPOONS CUMIN

1 TABLESPOON PAPRIKA

1 TEASPOON GROUND CORIANDER

SALT AND PEPPER, TO TASTE (BE A LITTLE MORE LIBERAL WITH THE SALT)

6 WOODEN SKEWERS

¼ CUP OLIVE OIL

Continued...

DIRECTIONS

1. To begin preparations for the kefta, place all of the ingredients, except for the olive oil and the skewers, in a mixing bowl and stir until well combined. Place a small bit of the mixture in a skillet and cook over medium heat until cooked through. Taste and adjust the seasoning as necessary. Form the mixture into 18 ovals and place three meatballs on each skewer.

2. Place the olive oil in a Dutch oven and warm over medium-high heat. Working in batches, add three skewers to the pot and sear the kefta for 2 minutes on each side until browned all over. Remove from the pot and set aside.

3. Return the skewers to the pot, cover, and remove it from heat. Let stand for 10 minutes so the kefta get cooked through.

4. When the kefta are cooked through, remove them from the skewers and set the kefta aside.

5. To prepare the salad, place all of the ingredients in a small mixing bowl and stir until combined. Place the salad on serving plates, top with the Kefta, and serve.

FOR THE SALAD

½ CUP GARBANZO BEANS, SOAKED
OVERNIGHT AND DRAINED

4 CUPS CHICKEN STOCK (SEE PAGE
30 FOR HOMEMADE)

½ ONION, DICED

½ CUP MINCED CILANTRO STEMS

2 TABLESPOONS OLIVE OIL

JUICE OF 1 LEMON

¼ TEASPOON SAFFRON

1 TABLESPOON CUMIN

1 TEASPOON CINNAMON

½ TEASPOON RED PEPPER FLAKES

SALT AND PEPPER, TO TASTE

Mulligatawny

YIELD: **4 SERVINGS**

ACTIVE TIME: **20 MINUTES**

TOTAL TIME: **1 HOUR**

The tenderness of the lamb and the incredible aroma of this soup make this classic Indian dish a surefire hit.

INGREDIENTS

4 TEASPOONS POPPY SEEDS

½ TEASPOON CUMIN SEEDS

1 TEASPOON CORIANDER SEEDS

¼ TEASPOON TURMERIC

1 YELLOW ONION, CHOPPED

4 GARLIC CLOVES, MINCED

1" PIECE OF GINGER, PEELED AND GRATED

¼ CUP OLIVE OIL

¾ LB. LAMB LOIN, CUT INTO ½" PIECES

PINCH OF CAYENNE PEPPER

4 CUPS BEEF STOCK (SEE PAGE 67 FOR HOMEMADE) OR WATER

¼ CUP LONG-GRAIN RICE

1 TABLESPOON FRESH LEMON JUICE

¼ CUP COCONUT MILK

SALT AND PEPPER, TO TASTE

SHREDDED COCONUT, FOR GARNISH

CILANTRO, CHOPPED, FOR GARNISH

DIRECTIONS

1. Place the poppy seeds, cumin seeds, and coriander seeds in a dry skillet and toast for 30 seconds over medium heat. Place the toasted seeds, turmeric, onion, garlic, ginger, and 2 tablespoons of the oil in a food processor or blender and puree until the mixture is a paste. Set aside.

2. Place the remaining oil in a saucepan and warm over medium-high heat. Add the lamb and cook, while stirring, until it is browned all over, about 8 minutes. Add the paste and cook for 2 minutes, while stirring constantly.

3. Add the cayenne pepper and stock or water and bring to a boil. Reduce heat so that the soup simmers, add the rice, and cook until the rice is tender, about 20 minutes.

4. Add the lemon juice and coconut milk, season with salt and pepper, and ladle into warmed bowls. Garnish with the coconut and cilantro and serve.

CHAPTER 5

SEAFOOD

Thanks to its ability to accommodate whatever seasoning one can come up with, seafood is beloved by the bold cook. Even the most pungent fish offer themselves up to everything from the lightest of spices to the most complex of marinades, both of which provide a striking contrast to the fresh, briny flavor afforded by the sea. But, since seafood tends to cook faster than the other proteins featured in this book, understanding how to bring flavor to dishes utilizing it becomes doubly important. Whether it be the haunting flavor of the Tea-Smoked Salmon (see page 140) or the colorful crunch supplied by the Dukkah-Spiced Sea Bass (see pages 146–147), this chapter goes deep to show you how to pay tribute to the bountiful gifts of the ocean.

Tea-Smoked Salmon

YIELD: **4 SERVINGS**

ACTIVE TIME: **10 MINUTES**

TOTAL TIME: **1 HOUR**

Smoking food brings a whole different dimension of flavor that's totally worth exploring. A brief kiss can add a haunting flavor, while a good long time in the smoker brings something wild and unctuous to the table.

INGREDIENTS

½ CUP OLIVE OIL, PLUS MORE AS NEEDED

½ CUP MIRIN

1 TABLESPOON BROWN SUGAR

1 TABLESPOON MINCED GINGER

1 TEASPOON ORANGE ZEST

1 LB. SKINLESS, CENTER-CUT SALMON FILLETS

1 CUP WHITE RICE

½ CUP GRANULATED SUGAR

1 CUP GREEN TEA (GUNPOWDER PREFERRED)

1 ORANGE PEEL, DICED

DIRECTIONS

1. In a shallow dish, whisk together the oil, mirin, brown sugar, ginger, and orange zest. Add the salmon and let marinate for 30 minutes.

2. Line a large wok with aluminum foil. You want the foil to extend over the sides of the wok. Add the rice, granulated sugar, tea, and orange peel to the wok and cook over high heat until the rice begins to smoke.

3. Place the salmon on a lightly oiled rack, set it above the smoking rice, and place the lid on top of the wok. Fold the foil over the lid to seal the wok as best as you can.

4. Reduce heat to medium and cook for 10 minutes.

5. Remove from heat and let the wok cool completely, about 20 minutes. When done, the fish will be cooked to medium. Serve immediately.

Teriyaki Salmon & Vegetables

YIELD: **4 SERVINGS**

ACTIVE TIME: **20 MINUTES**

TOTAL TIME: **20 MINUTES**

A great starting place if you've got a family full of folks who are wary of seafood.

INGREDIENTS

FOR THE TERIYAKI SAUCE

1 TABLESPOON MINCED GINGER

3 GARLIC CLOVES, MINCED

1 TABLESPOON RICE VINEGAR

2 TABLESPOONS BROWN SUGAR

¼ CUP SOY SAUCE

1 TABLESPOON CORNSTARCH

½ CUP WATER

FOR THE SALMON & VEGETABLES

3 TABLESPOONS OLIVE OIL

4 CHINESE EGGPLANTS, SLICED INTO ½" PIECES

1 RED BELL PEPPER, STEMMED, SEEDED, AND SLICED THIN

2 TABLESPOONS CHOPPED SCALLIONS

1 CUP BEAN SPROUTS

2 LBS. SALMON FILLETS

SALT AND PEPPER, TO TASTE

DIRECTIONS

1. To prepare the teriyaki sauce, place all of the ingredients in a blender and puree until smooth. Transfer to a 12" cast-iron skillet and cook, while stirring, over medium heat until the sauce starts to thicken. Remove from heat and set aside.

2. Wipe out the skillet and preheat your oven to 375°F. To prepare the salmon and vegetables, place the olive oil in the skillet and warm over medium-high heat. Add the eggplants, bell pepper, and scallions to the pan and cook, stirring occasionally, until the eggplants start to break down, about 5 minutes. Add the bean sprouts and stir to incorporate.

3. Place the salmon on top of the vegetables, skin-side down, season with salt, pepper, and some of the teriyaki sauce and transfer the pan to the oven. Bake until the salmon is cooked through, about 8 minutes, remove the pan from the oven, top with more teriyaki sauce, and serve.

Pickled Fried Herring

YIELD: **4 SERVINGS**

ACTIVE TIME: **20 MINUTES**

TOTAL TIME: **12 HOURS AND 30 MINUTES**

If you have access to very tender, young pine needles, they will add a bright, woodsy flavor to this rich, satisfying recipe.

INGREDIENTS

12 WHOLE HERRING, BUTTERFLIED AND BONED

½ CUP DIJON MUSTARD

1 STICK UNSALTED BUTTER

1 CUP SUGAR

1 CUP WATER

2 CUPS WHITE VINEGAR

2 TABLESPOONS KOSHER SALT

1 RED ONION, SLICED THIN

10 JUNIPER BERRIES

2 SPRIGS OF FRESH, YOUNG PINE NEEDLES (OPTIONAL)

6 WHOLE BLACK PEPPERCORNS

2 BAY LEAVES

½ CUP FRESH DILL, CHOPPED

BOILED NEW POTATOES, FOR SERVING

DARK RYE BREAD, TOASTED, FOR SERVING

DIRECTIONS

1. Brush the herring fillets with the mustard.

2. Place a large cast-iron skillet over medium heat and add the butter. When it is sizzling, add the fillets and cook, while turning once, until both sides are lightly browned, 2 to 3 minutes per side. Remove the fillets with a thin spatula and transfer them to a shallow baking dish.

3. Place the sugar and water in a saucepan and bring to a simmer over medium heat. Add the vinegar, salt, red onion, juniper berries, pine needles (if using), peppercorns, and bay leaves and let the mixture simmer for 2 minutes.

4. Pour the pickling liquid over the herring, sprinkle the dill over the fish, and let cool to room temperature. Cover the dish with plastic wrap and refrigerate for 12 hours or longer.

5. To serve, drain the fillets and serve with some of the pickling liquid and aromatics alongside the boiled potatoes and toasted rye bread.

DUKKAH

Yield: ¾ Cup   Active Time: 10 Minutes   Total Time: 10 Minutes

---

2 tablespoons pumpkin seeds

2 tablespoons hazelnuts or pistachios

2 tablespoons peanuts

1 teaspoon black peppercorns

1 tablespoon white sesame seeds

1 teaspoon dried mint

2 tablespoons minced thyme

1 teaspoon coriander seeds

1 teaspoon cumin seeds

2 teaspoons kosher salt

1. Place a large, dry cast-iron skillet over medium heat and add all of the ingredients other than the salt. Toast, while stirring continuously, until the seeds and nuts are lightly browned.

2. Remove from the heat and use a mortar and pestle, or a spice grinder, to grind the mixture into a powder. Make sure to not grind the mixture too much, as you do not want it to be a paste.

3. Add the salt and stir to combine. The mixture will keep in an airtight container for a month.

Dukkah-Spiced Sea Bass

YIELD: **4 SERVINGS**

ACTIVE TIME: **5 MINUTES**

TOTAL TIME: **20 MINUTES**

Dukkah is a Middle Eastern spice blend that's typically mixed with olive oil and served as a dip or used as a topping for hummus. But it can work in so many other recipes, such as scrambled eggs, salad dressing, and this perfect weeknight preparation.

INGREDIENTS

1½ LBS. SEA BASS FILLETS

2 TABLESPOONS DUKKAH (SEE SIDEBAR)

1 TABLESPOON OLIVE OIL

1 CUP PLAIN GREEK YOGURT

LARGE PINCH OF DRIED MINT

¼ CUP COCONUT OIL

6 CUPS FRESH SPINACH

LEMON WEDGES, FOR SERVING

DIRECTIONS

1. Pat the sea bass fillets dry with a paper towel. Place them on a plate and coat with a thick layer of the Dukkah. Let them stand at room temperature for 15 minutes.

2. Place the olive oil, yogurt, and mint in a bowl and stir to combine. Set the mixture aside.

3. Place a 12" cast-iron skillet over medium heat and add the coconut oil. When the oil starts to shimmer, add the sea bass and cook, while turning over once, until browned and cooked through, about 3 minutes per side.

4. Use a thin spatula to remove the fish from the pan and set it aside. Add the spinach and sauté until wilted, about 2 minutes.

5. Serve the fish with the spinach, a dollop of the mint-and-yogurt sauce, lemon wedges, and any remaining Dukkah.

Halibut with Braised Vegetables

YIELD: **4 SERVINGS**

ACTIVE TIME: **30 MINUTES**

TOTAL TIME: **1 HOUR**

The kale is key to this one, as it provides a nice soft bed for the halibut and ensures that it remains moist and full of flavor.

INGREDIENTS

¼ CUP OLIVE OIL

1 YELLOW BELL PEPPER, STEMMED, SEEDED, AND DICED

1 RED BELL PEPPER, STEMMED, SEEDED, AND DICED

1 HABANERO PEPPER, PIERCED

2 SMALL WHITE SWEET POTATOES

1 CUP DICED RED CABBAGE

3 GRAFFITI EGGPLANTS, CUT INTO 2" PIECES

2 TABLESPOONS MASHED GINGER

4 GARLIC CLOVES, MINCED

2 TABLESPOONS GREEN CURRY PASTE

3 BABY BOK CHOY, CHOPPED

4 CUPS FISH STOCK (SEE SIDEBAR)

2 TABLESPOONS SWEET PAPRIKA

2 TABLESPOONS CHOPPED FRESH CILANTRO

3 (14 OZ.) CANS OF COCONUT MILK

2 BUNCHES OF TUSCAN KALE, STEMS REMOVED, LEAVES TORN

1½ LBS. HALIBUT FILLETS

SALT AND PEPPER, TO TASTE

SCALLIONS, CHOPPED, FOR GARNISH

DIRECTIONS

1. Place the olive oil in a Dutch oven and warm over medium-high heat. When the oil starts to shimmer, add the bell peppers, habanero pepper, sweet potatoes, and cabbage. Season with salt and pepper and cook, while stirring, until the sweet potatoes begin to caramelize, about 6 minutes.

2. Add the eggplants, ginger, and garlic and cook, stirring frequently, until the eggplants begin to break down, about 10 minutes. Add the curry paste and stir to coat all of the vegetables. Cook until the mixture is fragrant, about 2 minutes.

3. Add the bok choy, stock, paprika, cilantro, and coconut milk and cook until the liquid has been reduced by one-quarter, about 20 minutes.

4. Add the kale to the Dutch oven. Place the halibut fillets on top of the kale, reduce the heat to medium, cover, and cook until the fish is cooked through, about 10 minutes.

5. Ladle the vegetables and the sauce into the bowls and top each portion with a halibut fillet. Garnish with the scallions and serve.

FISH STOCK

Yield: 6 Cups   Active Time: 20 Minutes   Total Time: 4 Hours

---

¼ cup olive oil

1 leek, trimmed, rinsed well, and chopped

1 large yellow onion, unpeeled, root cleaned, chopped

2 large carrots, chopped

1 celery stalk, chopped

¾ lb. whitefish bodies

4 sprigs of parsley

3 sprigs of thyme

2 bay leaves

1 teaspoon black peppercorns

1 teaspoon kosher salt

8 cups water

1. Place the olive oil in a stockpot and warm over low heat. Add the vegetables and cook until the liquid they release has evaporated. Add the whitefish bodies, the aromatics, the salt, and the water to the pot, raise the heat to high, and bring to a boil. Reduce heat so that the stock simmers and cook for 3 hours, while skimming to remove any impurities that float to the top.

2. Strain the stock through a fine sieve, let it cool slightly, and place in the refrigerator, uncovered, to chill. When the stock is completely cool, remove the fat layer from the top and cover. The stock will keep in the refrigerator for 3 to 5 days, and in the freezer for up to 3 months.

Cajun Tilapia

Tilapia, a firm-fleshed fish, is fairly bland and thus benefits from generous seasoning.

YIELD: **4 SERVINGS**

ACTIVE TIME: **10 MINUTES**

TOTAL TIME: **20 MINUTES**

INGREDIENTS

2 TABLESPOONS PAPRIKA

1 TABLESPOON ONION POWDER

3 TABLESPOONS GARLIC POWDER

2 TABLESPOONS CAYENNE PEPPER

1½ TEASPOONS CELERY SALT

1½ TABLESPOONS BLACK PEPPER

1 TABLESPOON DRIED THYME

1 TABLESPOON DRIED OREGANO

1 TABLESPOON GROUND CHIPOTLE

1 STICK UNSALTED BUTTER, MELTED

1 LB. BONELESS TILAPIA FILLETS

LEMON WEDGES, FOR SERVING

DIRECTIONS

1. Place the seasonings in a bowl, stir to combine, and set aside. Place the melted butter in a separate bowl.

2. Warm a 12" cast-iron skillet over high heat until it is extremely hot, about 10 minutes. While the skillet heats up, rinse the fillets and then pat dry with paper towels. Dip the fish fillets in the melted butter, covering both sides, and then press the blackened seasoning generously into both sides.

3. Place the fillets in the skillet and cook until cooked through, about 3 minutes per side. Baste the fillets with any remaining butter as they cook. Serve with lemon wedges.

Red Snapper with Tomatillo Sauce

YIELD: **4 SERVINGS**

ACTIVE TIME: **10 MINUTES**

TOTAL TIME: **10 MINUTES**

This recipe comes together in under 15 minutes, but it's still as joyous and awe-inspiring as a fireworks show on the Fourth of July.

INGREDIENTS

1 LB. TOMATILLOS, HUSKED, RINSED, AND QUARTERED

½ WHITE ONION, CHOPPED

1 SERRANO PEPPER, STEMMED

1 GARLIC CLOVE, CRUSHED

1 BUNCH OF FRESH CILANTRO, SOME LEAVES RESERVED FOR GARNISH

2 TABLESPOONS OLIVE OIL

1½ LBS. SKINLESS RED SNAPPER FILLETS

RADISH, SLICED, FOR GARNISH

GUACAMOLE (SEE PAGE 181), FOR SERVING

CORN TORTILLAS (SEE PAGE 68 FOR HOMEMADE), FOR SERVING

LIME WEDGES, FOR SERVING

DIRECTIONS

1. Place a dry skillet over high heat and add the tomatillos, onion, and serrano pepper. Cook until the vegetables are charred slightly, about 5 minutes, and then transfer them to a blender. Add the garlic and cilantro and puree until smooth.

2. Place the oil in a 12" cast-iron skillet and warm over medium-high heat. When the oil starts to shimmer, add the red snapper fillets in a single layer and cook until they brown slightly. Do not turn them over.

3. Remove the pan from heat and allow it to cool for a few minutes. Carefully pour the tomatillo sauce over the fish. It will immediately start to simmer. Place the skillet over medium heat and let it simmer until the fish is cooked through, about 4 minutes. Garnish with the reserved cilantro and sliced radish and serve with the Guacamole, tortillas, and lime wedges.

Swordfish with Citrus Salsa

YIELD: **4 SERVINGS**

ACTIVE TIME: **15 MINUTES**

TOTAL TIME: **1 HOUR AND 45 MINUTES**

Swordfish is often considered a meat lover's fish, and it's very filling. These swordfish steaks are delicious served with this citrus salsa.

INGREDIENTS

FOR THE SWORDFISH

JUICE OF ½ LEMON

¼ CUP FRESH BASIL LEAVES

1 GARLIC CLOVE, MINCED

½ CUP OLIVE OIL, PLUS MORE FOR THE GRILL

4 SWORDFISH STEAKS (EACH 1½" THICK)

SALT AND PEPPER, TO TASTE

FOR THE CITRUS SALSA

1 CUP DICED PINEAPPLE

¼ CUP DICED CUCUMBER

¼ CUP DICED MANGO

1 SMALL SHALLOT, CHOPPED

2 TABLESPOONS DICED BELL PEPPER

1 TABLESPOON MINCED FRESH CILANTRO

½ TABLESPOON FRESH LIME JUICE

½ TEASPOON TABASCO™

SALT AND PEPPER, TO TASTE

DIRECTIONS

1. To begin preparations for the swordfish, place the lemon juice, basil, and garlic in a bowl and stir to combine. Whisk in the olive oil and then let the marinade stand for 1 hour before using.

2. Rub the marinade over the swordfish steaks and then season with salt and pepper. Let stand at room temperature while you prepare the citrus salsa.

3. Preheat your gas or charcoal grill to high heat. To prepare the citrus salsa, place the pineapple, cucumber, mango, shallot, bell pepper, and cilantro in a large bowl and stir to combine. Stir in the lime juice and Tabasco™ and season with salt and pepper. Place the bowl in the refrigerator and chill until ready to serve.

4. When the grill is about 500°F, brush the grates with a little olive oil. Place the swordfish steaks on the grill and then grill until the fish is opaque, about 3 to 4 minutes per side.

5. Remove the steaks from the grill and let stand for 5 to 10 minutes before serving with the citrus salsa.

Grilled Tuna Steaks with Wasabi Butter

YIELD: **4 SERVINGS**

ACTIVE TIME: **15 MINUTES**

TOTAL TIME: **2 HOURS**

Convert those squeamish about sushi with this dish. The fish is seared, creating a savory crust that brings out tuna's buttery flavor.

INGREDIENTS

FOR THE WASABI BUTTER

1 STICK UNSALTED BUTTER, SOFTENED

1 TEASPOON PREPARED WASABI

½ TEASPOON KOSHER SALT

¼ TEASPOON SOY SAUCE

FOR THE TUNA

4 TUNA STEAKS (EACH 2" THICK)

2 TABLESPOONS OLIVE OIL, PLUS MORE AS NEEDED

2 TABLESPOONS BLACK PEPPER

2 TABLESPOONS KOSHER SALT

DIRECTIONS

1. To prepare the wasabi butter, place all of ingredients in a bowl and whisk until thoroughly combined. Cover the bowl with aluminum foil and refrigerate for at least 2 hours before serving.

2. To begin preparations for the tuna, rub the tuna steaks with a little olive oil and then season with the pepper and salt. Let stand at room temperature.

3. Preheat your gas or charcoal grill to high. When the grill is about 500°F, brush the grates with a little olive oil. Tuna steaks should always be cooked between rare and medium-rare; anything more will make them tough and dry. Place the tuna steaks directly over the hot part of the coals and sear for about 2 minutes per side. The tuna should be raw in the middle. Cook 2½ to 3 minutes per side for medium-rare.

4. Transfer the tuna steaks to a cutting board and let rest for 5 to 10 minutes. Slice against the grain and serve with the wasabi butter.

Spicy Mahi-Mahi

YIELD: **4 SERVINGS**

ACTIVE TIME: **15 MINUTES**

TOTAL TIME: **2 HOURS AND 30 MINUTES**

Because mahi-mahi has such a delicate taste, it works with nearly any side or marinade. Here, it acts as the ideal partner for the spice provided by the red pepper flakes and cayenne.

INGREDIENTS

½ CUP OLIVE OIL

JUICE OF ½ LIME

1 GARLIC CLOVE, MINCED

1 TEASPOON RED PEPPER FLAKES

½ TEASPOON CAYENNE PEPPER

1 LB. MAHI-MAHI FILLETS

SALT AND PEPPER, TO TASTE

DIRECTIONS

1. Place the olive oil, lime juice, garlic, red pepper flakes, and cayenne pepper in a baking pan and stir to combine. Place the mahi-mahi fillets in the marinade and let stand at room temperature for 1 to 2 hours, flipping them over once.

2. Preheat your gas or charcoal grill to medium-high heat.

3. When the grill is about 450°F, place the mahi-mahi fillets on the grill, cover the grill, and cook until the fillets are flaky and moist when touched with a fork, 4 to 5 minutes per side.

4. Remove the fillets from the grill, season with salt and pepper, and serve immediately.

Paella

YIELD: **4 TO 6 SERVINGS**

ACTIVE TIME: **40 MINUTES**

TOTAL TIME: **2 HOURS AND 15 MINUTES**

Sure, it's packed with chicken, sausage, and seafood, but the saffron is the true star of this meal. Its subtle, enigmatic flavor is certain to turn heads.

INGREDIENTS

½ CUP FRESH PARSLEY, CHOPPED

2 TABLESPOONS OLIVE OIL

1 LEMON, ½ JUICED AND ½ CUT INTO WEDGES

SALT AND PEPPER, TO TASTE

4 TO 6 BONELESS, SKINLESS CHICKEN THIGHS

16 TO 24 SHRIMP, SHELLED AND DEVEINED

½ LB. SPANISH CHORIZO

¼ CUP DICED PANCETTA

½ LARGE WHITE ONION, DICED

1 BELL PEPPER, MINCED

4 GARLIC CLOVES, MINCED

1 CUP DICED ROMA TOMATOES

3 CUPS SHORT-GRAIN RICE

6 CUPS CHICKEN STOCK (SEE PAGE 30 FOR HOMEMADE)

1 TEASPOON SAFFRON

1 TABLESPOON PIMENTON (SPANISH PAPRIKA)

16 TO 24 PEI MUSSELS, RINSED WELL AND DEBEARDED

1 CUP PEAS

DIRECTIONS

1. Preheat the oven to 450°F. Place 2 tablespoons of the parsley, the olive oil, lemon juice, salt, and pepper in a bowl and stir to combine. Add the chicken thighs to the bowl and marinate for 30 minutes to 1 hour.

2. Warm a cast-iron skillet over medium-high heat. Add the chicken to the pan and sear on each side for 3 to 5 minutes. Remove the chicken from the pan and set aside.

3. Place the shrimp in the pan and cook for 2 minutes on each side, until the shrimp is cooked approximately three-quarters of the way through. Remove the shrimp from the pan and set aside.

4. Place the chorizo, pancetta, onion, bell pepper, and half of the garlic in the skillet and cook until the onion is slightly caramelized, about 10 minutes. Season with salt and pepper and add the tomatoes, rice, stock, the remaining garlic and parsley, saffron, and pimenton. Cook for 10 minutes, while stirring often.

5. Reduce heat to medium-low and press the chicken into the mixture in the skillet. Cover the skillet and cook for 10 minutes.

6. Uncover the skillet and add the mussels, shrimp, and peas. Cover the skillet, place it in the oven, and cook until the majority of the mussels have opened and the rice is tender, about 12 minutes. Discard any mussels that have not opened. If the rice is still a bit crunchy, remove the mussels and shrimp, set them aside, return pan to the oven, and cook until the rice is tender.

Thai Mussels

The combination of sweet, sour, and spicy that Thai cuisine is famous for is on full display in this delightful and flavorful dish.

YIELD: **4 SERVINGS**

ACTIVE TIME: **15 MINUTES**

TOTAL TIME: **25 MINUTES**

INGREDIENTS

2 LBS. MUSSELS

⅔ CUP ALL-PURPOSE FLOUR

½ CUP FRESH CILANTRO

1 TABLESPOON OLIVE OIL

4 SHALLOTS, MINCED

2 GARLIC CLOVES, SLICED

1 LEMONGRASS STALK, CUT INTO 4 LARGE PIECES

1 BIRD'S EYE CHILI PEPPER, STEMMED, SEEDED, RIBBED, AND SLICED

1 (14 OZ.) CAN OF COCONUT MILK

1 TABLESPOON FISH SAUCE (OPTIONAL)

JUICE OF 1 LIME

½ LB. COOKED RICE NOODLES, FOR SERVING (OPTIONAL)

2 CUPS COOKED WHITE RICE, FOR SERVING (OPTIONAL)

DIRECTIONS

1. Place the mussels in a large bowl, cover with water, add the flour, and let soak for 30 minutes to ensure the mussels aren't sandy. Drain the mussels and debeard them.

2. Remove the cilantro leaves from the stems. Set the leaves aside and finely chop the stems.

3. Place the olive oil in a Dutch oven and warm over medium-high heat until it is shimmering. Add the shallots, garlic, chopped cilantro stems, lemongrass, and the bird's eye chili and cook, while stirring, until the garlic is lightly browned, about 3 minutes. Add the coconut milk and, if using, the fish sauce and bring to a boil.

4. Add the mussels and immediately cover the pot. Steam the mussels until the majority of them have opened and the meat is still plump, about 5 minutes. Be careful not to overcook the mussels, as it will cause them to have a rubbery texture. Discard any mussels that do not open.

5. Stir a few times to coat the mussels and add half of the lime juice. Taste and add more lime juice as needed. Ladle into warmed bowls and garnish with the reserved cilantro leaves. Serve with rice noodles or white rice.

Shrimp Curry

Yes, it's a long list of ingredients. But once you see how much flavor this has and how quickly it's ready, you won't even bat an eye.

INGREDIENTS

16 LARGE SHRIMP, SHELLED AND DEVEINED

1 CUP SHREDDED UNSWEETENED COCONUT

1 TEASPOON CUMIN SEEDS

3 CHILES DE ÁRBOL, STEMMED

2 LARGE TOMATOES, CHOPPED

¼ CUP OLIVE OIL

5 WHOLE CLOVES

4 GREEN CARDAMOM PODS

2 BAY LEAVES

1 CINNAMON STICK

1 YELLOW ONION, CHOPPED

1 TABLESPOON GROUND CORIANDER

1 TEASPOON TURMERIC

1 TEASPOON BLACK PEPPER

2 GARLIC CLOVES, MASHED

1 TEASPOON MASHED GINGER

1 (14 OZ.) CAN OF COCONUT MILK

½ CUP WATER

2 TABLESPOONS BROWN SUGAR

2 SERRANO PEPPERS, STEMMED, SEEDED, AND SLICED THIN

1 CUP FRESH CILANTRO, CHOPPED

SALT, TO TASTE

DIRECTIONS

1. Place four of the shrimp, the coconut, cumin seeds, chiles de árbol, tomatoes, and olive oil in a food processor and puree until the mixture is a paste.

2. Place the cloves, cardamom pods, bay leaves, and cinnamon stick in a dry 12" cast-iron skillet and cook over medium heat until fragrant, about 1 minute. Stir in the onion, coriander, turmeric, black pepper, garlic, and ginger. Cook for 1 minute, add the shrimp paste, and stir to combine. Cook, while stirring often, for 4 minutes.

3. Add the coconut milk and water and bring to a boil. Add the brown sugar and serrano peppers, stir to incorporate, and cook for another minute.

4. Reduce the heat, add the remaining shrimp and the cilantro, and simmer until the shrimp are pink and the sauce thickens slightly, 6 to 8 minutes. Season with salt and ladle into warmed bowls.

TIP: For a more authentic preparation, substitute jaggery, an unrefined sugar that typically comes from the sap of palm trees, for the brown sugar.

Garlic Shrimp

YIELD: **4 SERVINGS**

ACTIVE TIME: **5 MINUTES**

TOTAL TIME: **10 MINUTES**

What's not to like here? Sweet, briny shrimp, loads of luscious butter, and a bit of mellowed garlic, all held together by the acidic kick of lemon.

INGREDIENTS

4 TABLESPOONS UNSALTED BUTTER, AT ROOM TEMPERATURE

1 LB. SHRIMP, SHELLED AND DEVEINED

8 GARLIC CLOVES, MINCED

½ TEASPOON LEMON-PEPPER SEASONING

1 TABLESPOON FRESH LEMON JUICE

1 TEASPOON MINCED CHIVES OR PARSLEY, FOR GARNISH

DIRECTIONS

1. Place a 10" cast-iron skillet over medium heat and add the butter.

2. When the butter has melted and is bubbling, add the shrimp and cook, without stirring, for 3 minutes. Remove the shrimp from the pan with a slotted spoon and set them aside.

3. Reduce the heat to medium-low and add the garlic and lemon-pepper seasoning. Cook until the garlic has softened, about 3 minutes. Return the shrimp to the pan and cook until warmed through, about 1 minute. To serve, sprinkle the lemon juice on top and garnish with the chives or parsley.

Smoked Trout with Celeriac Remoulade

YIELD: **4 SERVINGS**

ACTIVE TIME: **10 MINUTES**

TOTAL TIME: **10 MINUTES**

This is a classic means of preparing celeriac; the grated root is combined with a tangy sauce and used as a base for seafood.

INGREDIENTS

SALT AND WHITE PEPPER, TO TASTE

2 LARGE CELERIAC, PEELED AND GRATED

⅔ CUP MAYONNAISE

DASH OF TABASCO™

1 TEASPOON DIJON MUSTARD

1 TABLESPOON FRESH LEMON JUICE

2 TEASPOONS CAPERS

1 HEAD OF BIBB LETTUCE

½ LB. SMOKED TROUT, TORN INTO LARGE PIECES

CHIVES OR PARSLEY, CHOPPED, FOR GARNISH

LEMON WEDGES, FOR SERVING

DIRECTIONS

1. Bring a saucepan of water to a boil and add a generous spoonful of salt. Add the celeriac and cook for 1 minute. Drain, rinse with cold water, and let it drain completely.

2. Place the mayonnaise, Tabasco™, mustard, lemon juice, and capers in a bowl and stir to combine.

3. Add the celeriac to the mayonnaise mixture, fold to combine, and season with salt and pepper.

4. Place a few lettuce leaves on each plate, place a mound of the remoulade on top, and top with a few pieces of the smoked trout. Garnish with chives or parsley and serve with lemon wedges on the side.

Jambalaya

Charring the sausage at the beginning of your preparation adds an indispensable smokiness to this Cajun classic.

YIELD: **6 SERVINGS**

ACTIVE TIME: **25 MINUTES**

TOTAL TIME: **1 HOUR AND 15 MINUTES**

INGREDIENTS

½ LB. ANDOUILLE SAUSAGE, SLICED

½ LB. SMALL SHRIMP, SHELLED AND DEVEINED

¼ CUP OLIVE OIL

4 BONELESS, SKINLESS CHICKEN THIGHS, CUT INTO 2" CUBES

2 YELLOW ONIONS, DICED

1 LARGE GREEN BELL PEPPER, STEMMED, SEEDED, AND DICED

2 CELERY STALKS, DICED

3 GARLIC CLOVES, MINCED

2 TO 3 PLUM TOMATOES, DICED

2 BAY LEAVES

2 TABLESPOONS PAPRIKA

2 TABLESPOONS DRIED THYME

1 TABLESPOON GRANULATED GARLIC

1 TABLESPOON GRANULATED ONION

Continued...

DIRECTIONS

1. Place the sausage in a Dutch oven and cook over medium-high heat. Cook for 2 minutes on each side, remove, and set aside. Add the shrimp and cook for 1 minute on each side. Remove and set aside.

2. Add the oil, chicken, onions, bell pepper, and celery. Cook, stirring occasionally, until the vegetables start to caramelize and the chicken is browned and cooked through, 6 to 8 minutes. Add the garlic and cook for another 2 minutes.

3. Add the tomatoes, the bay leaves, and all of the seasonings. Cook for 30 minutes and stir occasionally to prevent the contents of the Dutch oven from burning.

4. Add the rice, Worcestershire sauce, hot sauce, and stock. Return the sausage to the pot, reduce heat to medium-low, cover, and cook for 25 minutes.

5. Return the shrimp to the pot, cover, and cook for 5 minutes. Season with salt and pepper, ladle into bowls, and garnish with the scallions.

1 TEASPOON CAYENNE PEPPER

1½ CUPS LONG-GRAIN
WHITE RICE

2 TABLESPOONS WORCESTERSHIRE
SAUCE

HOT SAUCE, TO TASTE

3 CUPS CHICKEN STOCK (SEE
PAGE 30 FOR HOMEMADE)

SALT AND PEPPER, TO TASTE

SCALLIONS, CHOPPED,
FOR GARNISH

Scallops with Peaches & Basil-Cilantro Puree

YIELD: **4 TO 6 SERVINGS**

ACTIVE TIME: **30 MINUTES**

TOTAL TIME: **2 HOURS AND 30 MINUTES**

Although they seem small, scallops are extremely filling and do not require a large side to accompany them. A light salad, such as the Shaved Squash Salad with Herb Vinaigrette on page 221, will do the trick.

INGREDIENTS

FOR THE SCALLOPS

4 LARGE, RIPE PEACHES, PITTED AND DICED

2 TABLESPOONS OLIVE OIL

15 SCALLOPS

JUICE OF 1 LEMON WEDGE

SALT AND PEPPER, TO TASTE

FOR THE BASIL-CILANTRO PUREE

½ CUP CILANTRO LEAVES

½ CUP BASIL LEAVES

2 TABLESPOONS FLAT-LEAF PARSLEY LEAVES

2 GARLIC CLOVES, MINCED

2 TABLESPOONS MINCED JALAPEÑO PEPPER

JUICE OF ½ LIME

¼ CUP OLIVE OIL

SALT AND PEPPER, TO TASTE

DIRECTIONS

1. To begin preparations for the scallops, place the peaches and olive oil in a bowl and stir to combine. Let rest until the juices from the peaches cover the bottom of the bowl, about 30 minutes.

2. Season the scallops with the lemon juice, salt, and pepper and then place them in the peach mixture. Arrange the scallops so that most of them are covered by the liquid. Place in the refrigerator and marinate for 1 to 1½ hours.

3. Preheat your gas or charcoal grill to medium heat and designate a section for direct heat and another for indirect heat. To do so, simply pile the coals on one side of a charcoal grill or turn off one of the burners on a gas grill.

4. To prepare the puree, place the cilantro, basil, parsley, garlic, and jalapeño in a small food processor. Puree until the mixture is a thick paste and then slowly add the lime juice and olive oil until you reach the desired consistency. Season with salt and pepper and set aside.

5. When the grill is about 400°F, place the scallops over indirect heat. Cover the grill and cook until the scallops are firm and lightly charred, 2 to 3 minutes per side. Remove, let stand for 5 minutes, and serve with the basil-cilantro puree.

Lobster Tostadas with Corn Salsa & Cilantro-Lime Sour Cream

YIELD: 4 SERVINGS

ACTIVE TIME: 20 MINUTES

TOTAL TIME: 1 HOUR AND 30 MINUTES

Lobster and corn are natural partners, but charring the corn adds a bit of depth and mystery to this dish.

INGREDIENTS

FOR THE TOSTADAS & SALSA

2 EARS OF CORN, HUSKED

1 TABLESPOON OLIVE OIL

SALT AND PEPPER, TO TASTE

1 SMALL JALAPEÑO PEPPER, STEMMED, SEEDED, RIBS REMOVED, AND DICED, PLUS MORE FOR GARNISH

¼ CUP CHOPPED RED ONION

2 TEASPOONS MINCED GARLIC

1½ TABLESPOONS FRESH LIME JUICE

¼ CUP CHOPPED FRESH CILANTRO, PLUS MORE FOR GARNISH

½ CUP CHOPPED TOMATO

2 CUPS CANOLA OIL

8 CORN TORTILLAS (SEE PAGE 68 FOR HOMEMADE)

PAPRIKA, TO TASTE

MEAT FROM 4 COOKED CHICKEN LOBSTERS

Continued…

DIRECTIONS

1. Preheat your gas or charcoal grill to medium heat.

2. To begin preparations for the tostadas and salsa, drizzle the corn with the olive oil and season with salt and pepper. When the grill is 400°F, place the corn on the grill and cook, while turning, until charred all over, about 8 minutes. Remove from the grill and let cool.

3. When the corn is cool enough to handle, remove the kernels and place them in a mixing bowl. Add the jalapeño, onion, garlic, lime juice, cilantro, and tomato and stir to combine. Set the salsa aside.

4. To prepare the sour cream, place all of the ingredients in a mixing bowl, stir to combine, and set aside.

5. Place the canola oil in a Dutch oven and warm to 350°F over medium-high heat. Working with one tortilla at a time, place them into the oil and fry until golden brown. Remove from the oil, transfer to a paper towel-lined plate, and season with salt and paprika.

6. Spread some of the sour cream on each tortilla and top with the salsa and lobster meat. Garnish with jalapeño, cilantro, and red cabbage and serve with lime wedges.

FOR THE SOUR CREAM

½ CUP CHOPPED FRESH
CILANTRO

¼ CUP FRESH LIME JUICE

1¼ CUPS SOUR CREAM

1½ TEASPOONS KOSHER SALT

½ TEASPOON BLACK PEPPER

FOR GARNISH & SERVING

RED CABBAGE, CHOPPED

LIME WEDGES

Takoyaki

The perfect party food: unusual and delicious enough to impress and simple enough to partner with a nice, cold beer.

YIELD: **4 SERVINGS**

ACTIVE TIME: **20 MINUTES**

TOTAL TIME: **20 MINUTES**

INGREDIENTS

2 TEASPOONS SAKE

2 TEASPOONS MIRIN

2 TEASPOONS SOY SAUCE

2 TEASPOONS OYSTER SAUCE

2 TEASPOONS WORCESTERSHIRE SAUCE

1 TABLESPOON SUGAR

1 TABLESPOON KETCHUP

SALT AND WHITE PEPPER, TO TASTE

2 TABLESPOONS WATER, PLUS MORE AS NEEDED

1 LARGE EGG

1½ CUPS CHICKEN STOCK (SEE PAGE 30 FOR HOMEMADE)

¾ CUP ALL-PURPOSE FLOUR

1 CUP MINCED COOKED OCTOPUS

2 SCALLION GREENS, SLICED THIN

¼ CUP MINCED PICKLED GINGER

TAKOYAKI SAUCE (SEE SIDEBAR), FOR SERVING

DIRECTIONS

1. Place the sake, mirin, soy sauce, oyster sauce, Worcestershire sauce, sugar, ketchup, salt, and white pepper in a mixing bowl and stir to combine. Set the mixture aside.

2. Place the water, egg, and stock in a bowl and stir until combined. Sprinkle the flour over the mixture and stir until all of the flour has been incorporated and the mixture is a thick batter. Add the sake-and-mirin mixture and stir to incorporate. Pour the batter into a measuring cup with a spout.

3. Grease the wells of an aebleskiver pan with nonstick cooking spray and place it over medium heat. When the pan is hot, fill the wells of the pan halfway and add a pinch of octopus, scallion, and pickled ginger to each. Fill the wells the rest of the way with the batter, until they are almost overflowing. Cook the dumplings for approximately 2 minutes and use a chopstick to flip each one over. Turn the fritters as needed until they are golden brown on both sides and piping hot. Serve immediately alongside the Takoyaki Sauce.

NOTE: You can also use a cast-iron skillet to prepare the takoyaki, though they will not have the traditional round shape. To prepare them in a skillet, simply add the batter in ¼-cup portions, sprinkle the octopus, scallion, and pickled ginger on top, and use a thin spatula to flip them over.

TAKOYAKI SAUCE

½ cup Worcestershire sauce

1 tablespoon mentsuyu or chicken broth

2¼ teaspoons sugar

1½ teaspoons ketchup

1. Place all of the ingredients in a small bowl and whisk to combine. Taste, adjust the seasoning as needed, and serve.

CHAPTER 6

VEGETABLES

———

Those who exclude vegetable-based options from the list of "good" food are missing out on a whole world of possible flavors. From the blank slate of a block of fresh tofu to the crisp delight of blanched asparagus, there's plenty to be said for leaving the heavy tastes of animal proteins behind and drawing up a chair at the vegetables table. Even the simplest of vegetable meals, the salad, can become a showstopper when drizzled with the right dressing, and the staunchest of carnivores will find it hard to turn down Grilled Corn with Chipotle Mayonnaise & Goat Cheese (see page 200). Vegetables are so versatile that almost any seasoning blend, marinade, or sauce can be used to enhance your green of choice, making them the ultimate option when it comes to trying out new seasoning combinations. So head down to your local farm stand, and unlock the door to a world of unforgettable flavors.

Veggie Burgers

YIELD: **4 SERVINGS**

ACTIVE TIME: **15 MINUTES**

TOTAL TIME: **45 MINUTES**

When you want a break from meat but want the great taste and texture of a juicy hamburger, try making these.

INGREDIENTS

1 (14 OZ.) CAN OF BLACK BEANS, DRAINED AND RINSED

⅓ CUP MINCED SCALLIONS

¼ CUP ROASTED RED PEPPERS, CHOPPED

¼ CUP CANNED CORN

½ CUP PANKO BREAD CRUMBS

1 EGG, LIGHTLY BEATEN

2 TABLESPOONS CHOPPED FRESH CILANTRO

½ TEASPOON CUMIN

½ TEASPOON CAYENNE PEPPER

½ TEASPOON BLACK PEPPER

1 TEASPOON FRESH LIME JUICE

1 TABLESPOON OLIVE OIL

HAMBURGER BUNS, FOR SERVING

GUACAMOLE (SEE SIDEBAR), FOR SERVING

DIRECTIONS

1. Place half of the beans, the scallions, and roasted red peppers in a food processor and pulse until the mixture is a thick paste. Transfer to a large bowl.

2. Add the corn, bread crumbs, egg, cilantro, cumin, cayenne, black pepper, and lime juice to the bowl and stir to combine. Add the remaining beans and stir vigorously until the mixture holds together. Cover the bowl with plastic wrap and let it sit at room temperature for 30 minutes.

3. Place a 12" cast-iron skillet over medium-high heat and coat the bottom with the olive oil. Form the mixture into four patties. When the oil starts to shimmer, add the patties, cover the skillet, and cook until browned and cooked through, about 5 minutes per side. Serve immediately on hamburger buns with the Guacamole and your preferred toppings.

GUACAMOLE

3 avocados, halved, pitted, and peeled

Juice of 2 to 3 limes, plus more to taste

2 tomatoes, seeded and chopped

1 red onion, chopped

1 to 2 garlic cloves, minced

½ teaspoon kosher salt

Black pepper, to taste

Old Bay seasoning, to taste

1 tablespoon chopped fresh cilantro, for garnish

1. Place the avocados in a small bowl and mash roughly.

2. Add lime juice, tomatoes, onions, garlic, salt, pepper, and Old Bay seasoning. Fold until everything is incorporated and the mixture has reached the desired consistency. While a chunkier guacamole is easier for dipping, pureeing the mixture in a food processor gives it a smoother finish.

3. Garnish with cilantro, top with a final splash of lime juice, and serve.

Jerk Acorn Squash with Baby Kale Salad & Maple Vinaigrette

YIELD: **4 SERVINGS**

ACTIVE TIME: **25 MINUTES**

TOTAL TIME: **2 HOURS**

This dish is inspired by the irresistible flavor of jerk chicken. The melding of the sweet-savory taste of the acorn squash and the delicious spice of the jerk marinade is irresistible.

INGREDIENTS

FOR THE SQUASH & SALAD

2 ACORN SQUASH

JERK MARINADE (SEE SIDEBAR)

1 TABLESPOON OLIVE OIL

½ TEASPOON KOSHER SALT

¼ TEASPOON BLACK PEPPER

¼ TEASPOON PAPRIKA

6 CUPS BABY KALE

½ CUP DRIED CRANBERRIES

1 CUP CRUMBLED FETA CHEESE

FOR THE MAPLE VINAIGRETTE

½ CUP APPLE CIDER VINEGAR

½ CUP MAPLE SYRUP

1 TEASPOON ORANGE ZEST

2 TEASPOONS DIJON MUSTARD

1 TABLESPOON KOSHER SALT

Continued...

DIRECTIONS

1. Preheat the oven to 400°F.

2. To begin preparations for the squash and salad, cut the squash lengthwise, remove the seeds, and reserve them. Trim the ends of the squash so that each half can sit evenly, flesh-side up, on a baking sheet.

3. Score the flesh in a crosshatch pattern, cutting approximately ⅛" into the flesh. Brush some of the marinade on the squash and then fill the cavities with ⅓ cup.

4. Place the baking sheet in the oven and roast until the squash is tender, about 45 minutes to 1 hour. As the squash is cooking, brush the flesh with the marinade in the cavities every 15 minutes. Remove from the oven and let cool. Lower the oven temperature to 350°F.

5. Run the squash seeds under water and remove any pulp. Pat the seeds dry, place them in a mixing bowl, and add the olive oil, salt, pepper, and paprika. Toss to combine and then place the seeds on a baking sheet. Place in the oven and bake until they are light brown and crispy, about 7 minutes.

6. Place the toasted seeds, kale, and cranberries in a salad bowl and toss to combine.

Continued...

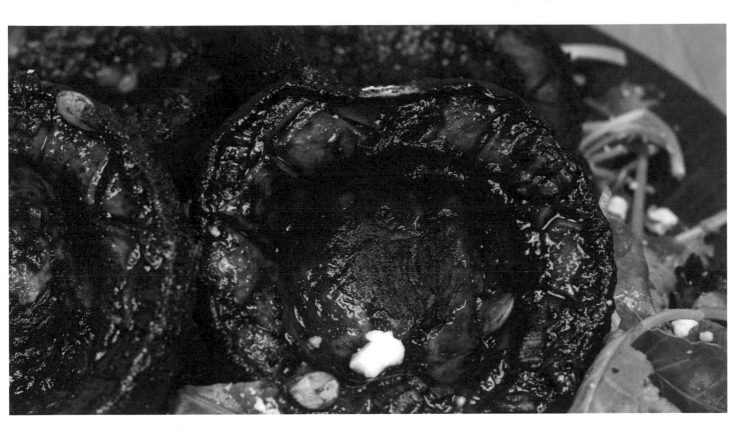

1 TEASPOON BLACK PEPPER

2 ICE CUBES (SEE PAGE 219 FOR NOTE ON ICE CUBES)

1½ CUPS OLIVE OIL

7. To prepare the vinaigrette, place all of the ingredients, except for the olive oil, in a blender. Turn on high and add the oil in a slow stream. Puree until the mixture has emulsified. Season to taste and add to the salad bowl. Toss to coat evenly and top the salad with the crumbled feta.

8. To serve, place a bed of salad on each plate and place one of the roasted halves of squash on top.

JERK MARINADE

¼ cup maple syrup	½ teaspoon nutmeg
¼ cup brown sugar	2 teaspoons kosher salt
1 tablespoon molasses	1 teaspoon black pepper
½ teaspoon cayenne pepper	2 teaspoons minced ginger
1 teaspoon chili powder	1 tablespoon chopped thyme leaves
1 teaspoon paprika	2 tablespoons sliced scallions
1 teaspoon cumin	2 tablespoons minced shallot
½ teaspoon ground cloves	2 garlic cloves, minced
1 teaspoon cinnamon	1 tablespoon fresh lime juice

1. Place all of the ingredients in a blender and puree until smooth.

Green Bean & Tofu Casserole

YIELD: **4 SERVINGS**

ACTIVE TIME: **5 MINUTES**

TOTAL TIME: **2 DAYS**

Slow roasting is the key here, as it concentrates everything the tofu soaked up while marinating.

INGREDIENTS

FOR THE MARINADE

3 TABLESPOONS SOY SAUCE

2 TABLESPOONS RICE VINEGAR

1 TABLESPOON SESAME OIL

1 TABLESPOON HONEY

PINCH OF CINNAMON

PINCH OF BLACK PEPPER

FOR THE CASSEROLE

1 (14 OZ.) PACKAGE OF EXTRA-FIRM TOFU, DRAINED AND CUT INTO 1" CUBES

1 LB. GREEN BEANS

4 OZ. SHIITAKE MUSHROOMS, SLICED

2 TABLESPOONS SESAME OIL

1 TABLESPOON SOY SAUCE

FOR GARNISH

2 TABLESPOONS SESAME SEEDS

DIRECTIONS

1. To prepare the marinade, place all of the ingredients in a small bowl and stir to combine.

2. To begin preparations for the casserole, place the tofu in a resealable plastic bag and add the tofu. Place the bag in the refrigerator and let marinate for 2 days.

3. Preheat the oven to 375°F. Remove the cubes of tofu from the resealable bag. Place the green beans, mushrooms, sesame oil, and soy sauce in the bag and shake until the vegetables are coated.

4. Line a 9 x 13-inch baking pan with parchment paper and place the tofu on it in an even layer. Place in the oven and roast for 35 minutes.

5. Remove the pan, flip the cubes of tofu over, and push them to the outer edge of the pan. Add the green bean-and-mushroom mixture, return the dish to the oven, and roast for 15 minutes, or until the green beans are cooked to your preference. Remove the pan from the oven, garnish with the sesame seeds, and serve.

Tofu Tacos with Avocado Crema

YIELD: **4 TO 6 SERVINGS**

ACTIVE TIME: **25 MINUTES**

TOTAL TIME: **50 MINUTES**

Tofu is largely tasteless, making it the perfect vehicle for your favorite seasonings. Make sure to give the tofu as much time to marinate as you can, as it will show in the end result.

INGREDIENTS

FOR THE TACOS

1 LB. EXTRA-FIRM TOFU, RINSED AND DRAINED

2 TABLESPOONS SMOKED PAPRIKA

1 TEASPOON CUMIN

1 TEASPOON GARLIC POWDER

JUICE OF 1 LIME

2 TABLESPOONS OLIVE OIL

15 TO 20 CORN TORTILLAS (SEE PAGE 68 FOR HOMEMADE)

1 SMALL RED ONION, CHOPPED

½ BUNCH OF CILANTRO, CHOPPED

1 PLUM TOMATO, CHOPPED

1 CUP CORN KERNELS

FOR THE AVOCADO CREMA

FLESH FROM 2 AVOCADOS

½ BUNCH OF CILANTRO, MINCED

2 GARLIC CLOVES, MINCED

1 SMALL JALAPEÑO PEPPER, STEMMED, SEEDED, AND MINCED

JUICE OF 1 LIME

3 TABLESPOONS OLIVE OIL

SALT AND PEPPER, TO TASTE

DIRECTIONS

1. Preheat your gas or charcoal grill to medium heat.

2. To begin preparations for the tacos, slice the tofu into rectangular strips (about 3" long) and place them in a bowl. Next, add the paprika, cumin, garlic powder, lime juice, and olive oil and toss so that the tofu is evenly coated. Let stand for at least 20 minutes.

3. To prepare the crema, place the avocados, cilantro, garlic cloves, jalapeño, lime juice, and olive oil in a food processor and pulse until smooth. Season with salt and pepper and set aside.

4. When the grill is about 400°F, place the marinated tofu strips on the grill and cook until grill marks appear on both sides of the tofu, about 2 minutes per side. Remove and set aside.

5. Place the tortillas on the grill. Cook them for about 20 to 30 seconds per side and then stack them on a plate. Let them rest for about 10 minutes or so. It is important to stack them in one pile since the tortillas will become too soft if they cool too much.

6. To serve, start with the tortillas at the bottom of the stack. Place a tortilla on a plate and then add the grilled tofu. Top with the onion, cilantro, tomato, and the corn. Serve with the crema on the side.

Sweet & Spicy Roasted Barley

YIELD: **4 SERVINGS**

ACTIVE TIME: **20 MINUTES**

TOTAL TIME: **1 HOUR AND 30 MINUTES**

This dish is light, sweet, spicy, and nutty. Considering how affordable all of the ingredients are, that's whole a lot of flavor for not very much money.

INGREDIENTS

5 CARROTS, PEELED AND CUT INTO 3" PIECES

OLIVE OIL, TO TASTE

SALT AND PEPPER, TO TASTE

6 DRIED PASILLA PEPPERS

2¼ CUPS BOILING WATER

1 CUP PEARL BARLEY

1 RED ONION, MINCED

2 TABLESPOONS ADOBO SEASONING

1 TABLESPOON SUGAR

1 TABLESPOON CHILI POWDER

¼ CUP DRIED OREGANO

DIRECTIONS

1. Preheat the oven to 375°F. Place the carrots in a 9 x 13-inch baking pan, drizzle with olive oil, and season with salt and pepper. Place in the oven and roast until the carrots are slightly soft to the touch, about 45 minutes.

2. While the carrots are cooking, open the Pasilla peppers and discard the seeds and stems. Place the peppers in a bowl, add the boiling water, and cover the bowl with aluminum foil.

3. When the carrots are cooked, remove the pan from the oven and add the remaining ingredients and the liquid the peppers have been soaking in. Chop the reconstituted peppers, add them to the pan, and spread the mixture so that the liquid is covering the barley. Cover the pan tightly with aluminum foil, place it in the oven, and roast until the barley is tender, about 45 minutes. Fluff with a fork and serve immediately.

Punjabi Samosa

YIELD: **16 SAMOSA**

ACTIVE TIME: **45 MINUTES**

TOTAL TIME: **1 HOUR AND 30 MINUTES**

Maida flour is finely milled to remove all of the bran from the wheat, producing a soft result that closely resembles cake flour.

INGREDIENTS

FOR THE WRAPPERS

2 CUPS MAIDA FLOUR, PLUS MORE FOR DUSTING

¼ TEASPOON KOSHER SALT

2 TABLESPOONS OLIVE OIL

½ CUP WATER, PLUS MORE AS NEEDED

FOR THE FILLING

2 RUSSET POTATOES, PEELED AND CHOPPED

2 TABLESPOONS VEGETABLE OIL, PLUS MORE FOR FRYING

1 TEASPOON CORIANDER SEEDS, CRUSHED

½ TEASPOON FENNEL SEEDS, CRUSHED

PINCH OF FENUGREEK SEEDS, CRUSHED

1 TABLESPOON MINCED GINGER

1 GARLIC CLOVE, MINCED

Continued...

DIRECTIONS

1. To begin preparations for the wrappers, place the flour and salt in a mixing bowl and use your hands to combine. Add the oil and work the mixture with your hands until it is a coarse meal. Add the water and knead the mixture until a smooth, firm dough forms. If the dough is too dry, incorporate more water, adding 1 tablespoon at a time. Cover the bowl with a kitchen towel and set aside.

2. To begin preparations for the filling, place the potatoes in a saucepan and cover with water. Bring the water to a boil and cook until fork-tender, about 20 minutes. Transfer to a bowl, mash until smooth, and set aside.

3. Place the oil in a skillet and warm over medium heat. Add the crushed seeds and cook until fragrant, about 2 minutes. Add the ginger, garlic, and jalapeño, stir-fry for 2 minutes, and then add the chili powder, coriander, turmeric, amchoor powder, and garam masala. Cook for another minute before adding the mashed potatoes and the curry leaves. Stir to combine, season with salt, transfer the mixture to a bowl and let it cool completely.

Continued...

1 TEASPOON MINCED
JALAPEÑO PEPPER

2 TEASPOONS CHILI POWDER

2 TABLESPOONS CORIANDER

¾ TEASPOON TURMERIC

1 TABLESPOON AMCHOOR POWDER

½ TEASPOON GARAM MASALA

6 CURRY LEAVES, MINCED

SALT, TO TASTE

4. Divide the dough for the wrappers into 8 pieces and roll each one out into a 6" circle on a flour-dusted work surface. Cut the circles in half and brush the flat edge of each with water. Fold one corner of the flat edge toward the other to make a cone and pinch to seal. Fill each cone one-third of the way with the filling, brush the opening with water, and pinch to seal. Place the sealed samosas on a parchment-lined baking sheet.

5. Add vegetable oil to a Dutch oven until it is 3" deep and heat it to 325°F over medium heat. Working in batches, add the filled samosas to the hot oil and fry, turning them as they cook, until they are golden brown, about 5 minutes. Transfer the cooked samosas to a paper towel-lined plate and serve once they have all been cooked.

Dudhi Kofta Curry

YIELD: **6 SERVINGS**

ACTIVE TIME: **30 MINUTES**

TOTAL TIME: **1 HOUR AND 30 MINUTES**

A great way to use up the surplus of zucchini that every summer seems to bring.

INGREDIENTS

FOR THE DUDHI KOFTA

2 LBS. ZUCCHINI, TRIMMED AND GRATED

2 TEASPOONS KOSHER SALT

1 SMALL RED ONION, CHOPPED

¼ CUP RAW CASHEWS

2 GARLIC CLOVES, MINCED

1 TABLESPOON MINCED GINGER

4 BIRD'S EYE CHILI PEPPERS, STEMMED, SEEDED, AND MINCED

½ CUP CHICKPEA FLOUR

2 TABLESPOONS MINCED FRESH CILANTRO

4 CUPS VEGETABLE OIL

FOR THE CURRY

2 TABLESPOONS OLIVE OIL

1 TEASPOON CUMIN SEEDS

1 RED ONION, CHOPPED

Continued...

DIRECTIONS

1. To begin preparations for the dudhi kofta, place the grated zucchini in a bowl, add the salt, and stir to combine. Let stand for 20 minutes.

2. Place the onion, cashews, garlic, ginger, and chilies in a food processor and pulse until the mixture becomes a chunky paste.

3. Place the zucchini on a clean kitchen towel and press down to remove as much liquid as possible. Place the zucchini in a mixing bowl and add the onion-and-cashew paste. Stir to combine, add the chickpea flour and cilantro, and fold to combine. The dough should be slightly wet.

4. To begin preparations for the curry, place the olive oil in a saucepan and warm over medium-high heat. Add the cumin seeds, cook until fragrant, and then add the onion, chilies, cashews, and raisins and cook until the onion and cashews are slightly browned, about 5 minutes. Add the tomatoes and salt and cook for another 2 minutes. Transfer the curry to a food processor and puree until smooth. Set aside.

Continued...

4 BIRD'S EYE CHILI PEPPERS, STEMMED, SEEDED, AND MINCED

2 TABLESPOONS RAW CASHEWS

2 TABLESPOONS GOLDEN RAISINS

1 (28 OZ.) CAN OF DICED TOMATOES

1 TEASPOON KOSHER SALT

¼ CUP WHOLE MILK

¼ CUP HEAVY CREAM

¼ TEASPOON GROUND TURMERIC

2 PINCHES OF GROUND PEPPER

2 PINCHES OF CINNAMON

2 PINCHES OF GROUND CLOVES

2 PINCHES OF NUTMEG

2 PINCHES OF GROUND CARDAMOM

5. To fry the dudhi kofta, place the vegetable oil in a Dutch oven and heat it to 300°F. As the oil warms, form tablespoons of the dough into balls and place them on a parchment-lined baking sheet. When the oil is ready, place the dumplings in the oil and fry until golden brown, about 5 minutes. Work in batches if necessary. Transfer the cooked dumplings to a paper towel–lined plate to drain.

6. Return the curry to the pan, add the remaining ingredients, and stir to combine. Heat until warmed through, ladle into warmed bowls, and top with the dudhi kofta.

Asparagus with Pancetta & Garlic Cream Sauce

YIELD: **4 SERVINGS**

ACTIVE TIME: **20 MINUTES**

TOTAL TIME: **35 MINUTES**

Asparagus has a unique, earthy flavor that teams with the richness of pancetta and the creamy garlic sauce to produce this well-rounded dish.

INGREDIENTS

SALT AND PEPPER, TO TASTE

2 BUNCHES OF ASPARAGUS

3 GARLIC CLOVES, MINCED

2 CUPS HEAVY CREAM

3 TABLESPOONS UNSALTED BUTTER

1 TABLESPOON CORNSTARCH

1 CUP DICED PANCETTA

DIRECTIONS

1. Bring a pot of salted water to a boil. While waiting for the water to boil, remove the woody, white parts of the asparagus and discard them. When the water is boiling, add the asparagus and cook until tender, about 2 minutes. Drain and set aside.

2. Place the garlic, cream, and butter in a medium saucepan and bring to a simmer over medium heat. Stir in the cornstarch to thicken the sauce and turn off the heat.

3. Place the pancetta in a skillet and cook, stirring frequently, over medium-high heat until it browns slightly, about 4 minutes. Add the pancetta to the sauce and stir to combine. Season with salt and pepper, pour over the asparagus, and serve.

Spicy Baby Carrots with Toasted Seed Granola

YIELD: **6 SERVINGS**

ACTIVE TIME: **30 MINUTES**

TOTAL TIME: **2 HOURS**

This spice blend is similar to what you would find in a barbecue rub, and it works wonderfully with the sweetness of carrots.

INGREDIENTS

2 LBS. BABY-CUT CARROTS

2 TABLESPOONS OLIVE OIL

2 TABLESPOONS KOSHER SALT

1 TEASPOON BLACK PEPPER

2 TEASPOONS CUMIN

1 TEASPOON GROUND FENNEL

1 TEASPOON CORIANDER

1 TEASPOON PAPRIKA

2 TEASPOONS BROWN SUGAR

TOASTED SEED GRANOLA, FOR SERVING (SEE SIDEBAR)

DIRECTIONS

1. Preheat the oven to 375°F. Place all of the ingredients, except for the granola, in a mixing bowl and toss to coat.

2. Place the carrots in an even layer in a 9 x 13-inch baking pan. Place in the oven and roast until the carrots are tender, about 25 minutes. Remove and let cool slightly before sprinkling the granola over the carrots and serving.

TOASTED SEED GRANOLA

1 tablespoon maple syrup

2 tablespoons honey

2 tablespoons brown sugar

2 tablespoons olive oil

1 teaspoon kosher salt

1½ cups oats

½ cup dried cranberries

¾ cup toasted squash seeds

1. Preheat the oven to 300°F. Place the syrup, honey, brown sugar, oil, and salt in a small saucepan and warm over medium heat, while stirring, until the sugar has dissolved.

2. Place the oats in a mixing bowl, add the warm honey mixture, and stir until the oats are evenly coated. Transfer to a parchment–lined baking sheet, place it in the oven, and roast for 40 minutes, stirring the mixture every 10 minutes.

3. Remove from the oven and let cool slightly. Transfer to a mixing bowl, fold in the cranberries and toasted squash seeds, and serve.

Zucchini Fritters with Sumac Yogurt

YIELD: **4 SERVINGS**

ACTIVE TIME: **15 MINUTES**

TOTAL TIME: **1 HOUR AND 30 MINUTES**

Zucchini has a number of wonderful uses, and turning it into fritters is one of the easiest ways to get people excited about it.

INGREDIENTS

FOR THE FRITTERS

1½ LBS. ZUCCHINI

SALT AND PEPPER, TO TASTE

¼ CUP ALL-PURPOSE FLOUR

¼ CUP GRATED PARMESAN CHEESE

1 EGG, BEATEN

3 TABLESPOONS OLIVE OIL

FOR THE SUMAC YOGURT

1 CUP YOGURT

2 TEASPOONS FRESH LEMON JUICE

2 TABLESPOONS SUMAC POWDER

SALT AND PEPPER, TO TASTE

DIRECTIONS

1. To begin preparations for the yogurt, line a colander with cheesecloth and grate the zucchini into the colander. Generously sprinkle with salt, stir to combine, and let sit for 1 hour. After 1 hour, press down on the zucchini to remove as much liquid from it as you can.

2. Place the zucchini, flour, Parmesan, and egg in a mixing bowl and stir to combine. Use your hands to form handfuls of the mixture into balls and then gently press down on the balls to form them into patties.

3. Place the oil in a cast-iron skillet and warm over medium-high heat. Working in batches, place the patties into the oil, taking care not to crowd the skillet. Cook until golden brown, about 5 minutes. Flip them over and cook for another 5 minutes, until the fritters are also golden brown on that side. Remove from the skillet, transfer to a paper towel–lined plate, and repeat with the remaining patties.

4. To prepare the sumac yogurt, place all of the ingredients in a small bowl and stir to combine.

5. Season the fritters with salt and pepper and serve alongside the sumac yogurt.

Grilled Corn with Chipotle Mayonnaise & Goat Cheese

YIELD: **6 SERVINGS**

ACTIVE TIME: **25 MINUTES**

TOTAL TIME: **1 HOUR AND 15 MINUTES**

This dish has got it all—sweet corn, spice from the chipotle, and a soft, creamy landing thanks to the goat cheese.

INGREDIENTS

6 EARS OF CORN

3 CHIPOTLE PEPPERS EN ADOBO

½ CUP MAYONNAISE

¼ CUP SOUR CREAM

1½ TABLESPOONS BROWN SUGAR

1 TABLESPOON FRESH LIME JUICE

2 TABLESPOONS CHOPPED FRESH CILANTRO, PLUS MORE FOR GARNISH

1 TEASPOON KOSHER SALT, PLUS MORE TO TASTE

½ TEASPOON BLACK PEPPER, PLUS MORE TO TASTE

3 TABLESPOONS OLIVE OIL

½ CUP CRUMBLED GOAT CHEESE

LIME WEDGES, FOR SERVING

DIRECTIONS

1. Preheat the oven to 400°F.

2. Place the ears of corn on a baking sheet, place it in the oven, and roast for 25 minutes, until the kernels have a slight give to them. Remove from the oven and let cool. When the ears of corn are cool enough to handle, remove the husks and silk.

3. Preheat your gas or charcoal grill to medium heat. Place the chipotles, mayonnaise, sour cream, brown sugar, lime juice, cilantro, salt, and pepper in a food processor and puree until smooth. Set aside.

4. When the grill is about 400°F, drizzle the corn with olive oil, season with salt and pepper, and place on the grill. Cook, while turning, until they are charred all over.

5. Spread the mayonnaise on the corn, sprinkle the goat cheese on top, and garnish with additional cilantro. Serve with wedges of lime.

HOT HONEY

Yield: 1 Cup   Active Time: 10 Minutes   Total Time: 2 Hours

4 hot chili peppers

1 cup honey

1. Place the chili peppers and honey in a saucepan and bring to a very gentle simmer over medium-low heat. Reduce heat to lowest possible setting and cook for 1 hour.

2. Remove the saucepan from heat and let the mixture infuse for another hour.

3. Remove the peppers. Transfer the honey to a container, cover, and store in the refrigerator.

NOTE: Fresno and cayenne peppers produce the best results. If you're after additional heat, use habanero peppers.

Roasted Brussels Sprouts with Hot Honey & Hazelnuts

YIELD: **4 SERVINGS**

ACTIVE TIME: **10 MINUTES**

TOTAL TIME: **50 MINUTES**

Don't be afraid to branch out into spicier peppers for the hot honey, as the sweetness of the honey balances the heat incredibly well.

INGREDIENTS

1½ LBS. BRUSSELS SPROUTS

3 TABLESPOONS OLIVE OIL

SALT AND PEPPER, TO TASTE

½ CUP HOT HONEY (SEE SIDEBAR)

½ CUP CHOPPED HAZELNUTS

½ CUP GRATED PARMESAN CHEESE

DIRECTIONS

1. Preheat the oven to 400°F.

2. Trim the ends of the Brussels sprouts and then cut them in half. Place them in a bowl with the oil and salt and toss to combine. Transfer the Brussels sprouts to a baking sheet, place them in the oven, and roast until they darken, about 30 to 40 minutes.

3. Remove the Brussels sprouts from the oven and let them cool slightly. Place them in a mixing bowl, add the honey, hazelnuts, and Parmesan and toss to combine. Season with salt and pepper and serve.

Garlic & Chili Broccolini

YIELD: **4 SERVINGS**

ACTIVE TIME: **15 MINUTES**

TOTAL TIME: **15 MINUTES**

You can make this with broccoli, but the sweeter flavor of broccolini is a better match for the spice.

INGREDIENTS

½ LB. BROCCOLINI, TRIMMED

¼ CUP OLIVE OIL

2 GARLIC CLOVES, MINCED

SALT AND PEPPER, TO TASTE

1 TEASPOON RED PEPPER FLAKES

2 TABLESPOONS TOASTED ALMONDS, FOR GARNISH

DIRECTIONS

1. Bring water to a boil in a medium saucepan. Add the broccolini and cook for 30 seconds. Drain and transfer the broccolini to a paper towel–lined plate.

2. Warm a skillet over medium-high heat and add the olive oil.

3. When the oil starts to smoke, add the broccolini and cook until well browned. Turn the broccolini over, add the garlic, season with salt and pepper, and toss to combine. When the broccolini is browned all over, add the red pepper flakes and toss to evenly distribute. Transfer to a serving platter, garnish with the toasted almonds, and serve immediately.

Roasted Cauliflower au Gratin

YIELD: **2 SERVINGS**

ACTIVE TIME: **20 MINUTES**

TOTAL TIME: **1 HOUR AND 15 MINUTES**

One surefire way to get people excited about cauliflower is poaching it in a flavorful stock and then carmelizing mild, nutty cheeses like Emmental and Parmesan on top.

INGREDIENTS

2 CUPS WHITE WINE

2½ CUPS WATER

⅓ CUP KOSHER SALT

2 STICKS UNSALTED BUTTER

6 GARLIC CLOVES, CRUSHED

2 SHALLOTS, HALVED

1 CINNAMON STICK

3 WHOLE CLOVES

1 TEASPOON BLACK PEPPERCORNS

1 SPRIG OF SAGE

2 SPRIGS OF THYME

1 HEAD OF CAULIFLOWER, LEAVES AND STALK REMOVED

1 CUP SHREDDED EMMENTAL CHEESE

¼ CUP GRATED PARMESAN CHEESE

DIRECTIONS

1. Place all of the ingredients, except for the cauliflower and cheeses, in a large saucepan and bring to a boil. Reduce heat so that the mixture simmers gently, add the head of cauliflower, and poach until tender, about 30 minutes.

2. While the cauliflower is poaching, preheat the oven to 450°F. Transfer the poached cauliflower to a baking sheet, place it in the oven, and roast until the top is a deep golden brown, about 10 minutes.

3. Remove from the oven and spread the cheeses evenly over the top. Return to the oven and roast until the cheeses have browned. Remove from the oven and let cool slightly before cutting it in half and serving.

Spicy Pickles

YIELD: **12 CUPS**

ACTIVE TIME: **20 MINUTES**

TOTAL TIME: **3 HOURS**

A refreshing and delicious preparation that you can confidently bring to the table no matter what else it contains.

INGREDIENTS

1 LB. PICKLING CUCUMBERS, SLICED THIN

1 SMALL YELLOW ONION, SLICED THIN

½ RED BELL PEPPER, STEMMED, SEEDED, AND SLICED THIN

1 HABANERO PEPPER, STEMMED, SEEDED, AND SLICED THIN

1 GARLIC CLOVE, SLICED

1 CUP SUGAR

1 CUP APPLE CIDER VINEGAR

2 TEASPOONS MUSTARD SEEDS

½ TEASPOON TURMERIC

PINCH OF BLACK PEPPER

⅓ CUP CANNING & PICKLING SALT

DIRECTIONS

1. Place the cucumbers, onion, peppers, and garlic in a large bowl and stir to combine.

2. Place the sugar, apple cider vinegar, mustard seeds, turmeric, and black pepper in a large saucepan and bring to a boil over medium-high heat, while stirring to dissolve the sugar.

3. Add the vegetables and the salt and return to a boil. Remove the pot from heat and let it cool slightly. Fill sterilized mason jars with the vegetables and cover with the brine. Let cool completely before sealing and placing in the refrigerator. The pickles will keep in the refrigerator for up to 2 weeks.

Melon, Cucumber & Prosciutto Salad with Mint Vinaigrette

YIELD: **4 TO 6 SERVINGS**

ACTIVE TIME: **15 MINUTES**

TOTAL TIME: **45 MINUTES**

The versatile melon can comfortably straddle the sweet-and-savory divide. Here it cozies up beside crispy, cured prosciutto and creamy feta to carry this dynamic salad.

INGREDIENTS

FOR THE SALAD

8 SLICES OF PROSCIUTTO

3 CUPS DICED CANTALOUPE

3 CUPS DICED HONEYDEW MELON

2 CUPS SLICED CUCUMBER

SALT AND PEPPER, TO TASTE

1 JALAPEÑO PEPPER, STEMMED, SEEDED, AND SLICED

⅔ CUP CRUMBLED FETA CHEESE

MINT LEAVES, CHOPPED, FOR GARNISH

FOR THE VINAIGRETTE

3 TABLESPOONS CHOPPED MINT

¼ CUP OLIVE OIL

3 TABLESPOONS APPLE CIDER VINEGAR

1 TABLESPOON HONEY

2 TEASPOONS DICED SHALLOT

1 TEASPOON KOSHER SALT

¼ TEASPOON PEPPER

DIRECTIONS

1. To begin preparations for the salad, preheat the oven to 350°F. Place the prosciutto on a parchment-lined baking sheet. Cover with another sheet of parchment and place another baking sheet that is the same size on top. Place in the oven and bake until the prosciutto is crisp, about 12 minutes. Remove from the oven and let cool. When the prosciutto is cool enough to handle, chop it into bite-sized pieces.

2. To prepare the vinaigrette, place all of the ingredients in a mixing bowl and whisk until thoroughly combined. Set aside.

3. Place the cantaloupe, honeydew melon, and cucumber in a salad bowl, season with salt and pepper, and toss to combine. Add the jalapeño and vinaigrette and toss until evenly coated. Plate the salad, top with the chopped prosciutto and feta, and garnish with mint leaves.

Chilled Corn Salad

YIELD: **4 SERVINGS**

ACTIVE TIME: **15 MINUTES**

TOTAL TIME: **4 TO 24 HOURS**

This recipe is a riff on a classic Mexican dish known as esquites, *and it can easily be altered to suit your family's taste and the changing seasons.*

INGREDIENTS

---

2 CUPS CORN KERNELS

2 TABLESPOONS UNSALTED BUTTER

1 POBLANO PEPPER, STEMMED, SEEDED, AND DICED

2 TABLESPOONS MAYONNAISE

2 TEASPOONS GARLIC POWDER

3 TABLESPOONS SOUR CREAM

¼ TEASPOON CAYENNE PEPPER

¼ TEASPOON CHILI POWDER

2 TABLESPOONS FETA CHEESE

2 TABLESPOONS COTIJA CHEESE

2 TEASPOONS FRESH LIME JUICE

½ CUP CHOPPED FRESH CILANTRO

SALT AND PEPPER, TO TASTE

4 CUPS LETTUCE OR ARUGULA

DIRECTIONS

---

1. Preheat the oven to 400°F. Place the corn on a baking sheet, place it in the oven, and bake until it turns a light golden brown, about 35 minutes.

2. Remove the corn from the oven, let it cool slightly, and then transfer to a large mixing bowl. Add all of the remaining ingredients, except for the lettuce or arugula, and stir to combine.

3. Place the salad in the refrigerator and chill for at least 3 hours, although letting it chill overnight is highly recommended. When ready to serve, add the lettuce or arugula and stir to incorporate.

Chili-Dusted Cauliflower & Chickpea Salad

YIELD: **4 TO 6 SERVINGS**

ACTIVE TIME: **25 MINUTES**

TOTAL TIME: **45 MINUTES**

Crunchy cauliflower, nutty chickpeas, and a perfect balance of sweet and spicy make this salad feel anything but thrown together.

INGREDIENTS

FOR THE SALAD

1 (14 OZ.) CAN OF CHICKPEAS, DRAINED AND RINSED

3 CUPS CHOPPED CAULIFLOWER FLORETS

3 GARLIC CLOVES, SLICED THIN

1 SHALLOT, SLICED THIN

⅓ CUP OLIVE OIL

½ TEASPOON DARK CHILI POWDER

½ TEASPOON CHIPOTLE POWDER

½ TEASPOON BLACK PEPPER

½ TEASPOON ONION POWDER

½ TEASPOON GARLIC POWDER

¼ TEASPOON PAPRIKA

1 TABLESPOON KOSHER SALT

Continued...

DIRECTIONS

1. Preheat the oven to 400°F.

2. To prepare the salad, place all of the ingredients in a mixing bowl and toss to coat. Place the mixture in a 9 x 13-inch baking pan, place the pan in the oven, and bake until the cauliflower is slightly charred and still crunchy, about 30 minutes. Let the mixture cool slightly.

3. To prepare the dressing, place all of the ingredients in a large mixing bowl and stir until the sugar is dissolved. Place the cooked cauliflower-and-chickpea mixture in the bowl, toss to coat, and serve.

FOR THE DRESSING

2 SCALLIONS, SLICED THIN

2 FRESNO PEPPERS, STEMMED,
SEEDED, AND SLICED THIN

3 TABLESPOONS SUGAR

¼ CUP RED WINE VINEGAR

½ TEASPOON DARK CHILI POWDER

½ TEASPOON CHIPOTLE POWDER

½ TEASPOON BLACK PEPPER

½ TEASPOON ONION POWDER

½ TEASPOON GARLIC POWDER

¼ TEASPOON PAPRIKA

½ TABLESPOON KOSHER SALT

Spring Salad with Green Goddess Dressing

The divine moniker is no accident—this dressing is robust enough to lend body to this light salad, but delicate enough to highlight the fresh herbs that comprise it.

INGREDIENTS

FOR THE DRESSING

½ CUP MAYONNAISE

⅔ CUP BUTTERMILK

1 TABLESPOON FRESH LEMON JUICE

2 TABLESPOONS CHOPPED CELERY LEAVES

2 TABLESPOONS CHOPPED FRESH PARSLEY

2 TABLESPOONS CHOPPED TARRAGON

2 TABLESPOONS SLICED CHIVES

2 TEASPOONS KOSHER SALT

1 TEASPOON BLACK PEPPER

FOR THE SALAD

SALT AND PEPPER, TO TASTE

6 ASPARAGUS STALKS, TRIMMED AND CHOPPED

4 OZ. SNAP PEAS, TRIMMED AND CHOPPED

3 HEADS OF BABY RED LEAF LETTUCE, HALVED

3 RADISHES, SLICED THIN WITH A MANDOLINE, FOR GARNISH

CELERY LEAVES, FOR GARNISH

DIRECTIONS

1. To prepare the dressing, place all of the ingredients in a food processor and puree until smooth and thoroughly combined. Transfer to a container and place in the refrigerator until ready to serve.

2. To begin preparations for the salad, bring a pot of salted water to a boil and prepare an ice water bath in a large bowl. Place the asparagus in the boiling water, cook for 1 minute, remove with a strainer, and transfer to the ice water bath until completely cool. Drain and transfer to a kitchen towel to dry.

3. Let the water come back to a boil. Place the peas in the boiling water, cook for 1 minute, remove with a strainer, and transfer to the ice water bath until completely cool. Transfer to a kitchen towel to dry.

4. Place the halved heads of lettuce on the serving plates. Place the asparagus and peas in a bowl, season with salt and pepper, and add some of the dressing. Toss to combine and place the dressed vegetables on top of the lettuce. Drizzle with additional dressing and garnish with the radishes and celery leaves.

Summer Salad with Oregano Vinaigrette

YIELD: **4 TO 6 SERVINGS**

ACTIVE TIME: **10 MINUTES**

TOTAL TIME: **20 MINUTES**

As this stripped-down salad shows, when you've got an ingredient as good as fresh tomatoes, you do all you can to stay out of its way.

INGREDIENTS

FOR THE VINAIGRETTE

¼ CUP CHAMPAGNE VINEGAR

½ SHALLOT

1 TEASPOON DIJON MUSTARD

2 TABLESPOONS HONEY

1 TEASPOON KOSHER SALT

¼ TEASPOON BLACK PEPPER

2 ICE CUBES

¾ CUP OLIVE OIL

1 TABLESPOON CHOPPED OREGANO

FOR THE SALAD

3 HEADS OF ROMAINE LETTUCE, CHOPPED

2 HEIRLOOM TOMATOES, DICED

1 CUCUMBER, DICED

SALT AND PEPPER, TO TASTE

PARMESAN CHEESE, SHAVED, FOR GARNISH

DIRECTIONS

1. To prepare the vinaigrette, place all of the ingredients, except for the oil and oregano, in a blender. Puree, starting on low speed and increasing to high, and add the oil in a slow stream. When the mixture is emulsified, transfer to a mixing bowl, add the oregano, and stir to incorporate. Season to taste and set aside.

2. To prepare the salad, place the lettuce, tomatoes, and cucumber in a large mixing bowl. Season with salt and pepper and add ½ cup of the vinaigrette. Toss to combine, taste, and season with more of the vinaigrette, if desired. Plate and garnish with the shaved Parmesan.

NOTE: You may be confused by the inclusion of the ice cubes in the vinaigrette, but it is necessary to ensure that the mixture does not get too warm in the blender, which would prevent it from emulsifying.

Shaved Squash Salad with Herb Vinaigrette

Shaved squash and a fresh-tasting vinaigrette make this salad a graceful start to a special meal.

INGREDIENTS

FOR THE SALAD

1 PINT CHERRY TOMATOES

1 TABLESPOON OLIVE OIL

5 GARLIC CLOVES, CRUSHED

LEAVES FROM 2 SPRIGS OF THYME

½ TEASPOON KOSHER SALT, PLUS MORE TO TASTE

¼ TEASPOON BLACK PEPPER, PLUS MORE TO TASTE

3 ZUCCHINI, SLICED THIN WITH A MANDOLINE

2 SUMMER SQUASH, SLICED THIN WITH A MANDOLINE

1 RED BELL PEPPER, STEMMED, SEEDED, AND SLICED THIN WITH A MANDOLINE

FOR THE VINAIGRETTE

1 TABLESPOON SLICED CHIVES

1 TEASPOON CHOPPED THYME

1 TEASPOON CHOPPED OREGANO

1 TABLESPOON CHOPPED PARSLEY

3 TABLESPOONS APPLE CIDER VINEGAR

1 TABLESPOON HONEY

2 TEASPOONS DICED SHALLOT

1 TEASPOON KOSHER SALT

¼ TEASPOON BLACK PEPPER

¼ CUP OLIVE OIL

DIRECTIONS

1. To begin preparations for the salad, preheat the broiler to high. Place the cherry tomatoes, olive oil, garlic, thyme, salt, and pepper in a mixing bowl and toss until the tomatoes are evenly coated. Place the tomatoes on a baking sheet, place in the oven, and broil until the skins begin to burst, 6 to 8 minutes. Remove from the oven and let cool completely.

2. To prepare the vinaigrette, place all of the ingredients, except for the olive oil, in a mixing bowl and whisk to combine. Add the oil in a slow stream while whisking to incorporate. Season to taste and set aside.

3. Place the zucchini, squash, and pepper in a large mixing bowl, season with salt and pepper, and add the vinaigrette. Toss to evenly coat, plate the salad, and sprinkle the blistered tomatoes over the top.

Sofrito & Quinoa Salad

YIELD: **4 SERVINGS**

ACTIVE TIME: **15 MINUTES**

TOTAL TIME: **4 HOURS**

This twist on traditional Spanish rice gives you the flavor you crave while adding protein in the form of quinoa and pumpkin seeds.

INGREDIENTS

2 POBLANO PEPPERS, STEMMED AND SEEDED

1 RED BELL PEPPER, STEMMED AND SEEDED

1 GREEN BELL PEPPER, STEMMED AND SEEDED

1 WHITE ONION, PEELED AND CUT INTO QUARTERS

3 PLUM TOMATOES

2 GARLIC CLOVES, PEELED

1 TABLESPOON CUMIN

2 TABLESPOONS ADOBO SEASONING

1½ CUPS QUINOA, RINSED

TOASTED PUMPKIN SEEDS, FOR GARNISH

DIRECTIONS

1. Dice one of the poblanos, half of the bell peppers, and half of the onion. Place these to the side. Add the remaining ingredients, except for the quinoa and the pumpkin seeds, to a blender or food processor and puree until smooth.

2. Place the diced vegetables, the puree, and the quinoa in a slow cooker and cook on low until the quinoa is fluffy, about 4 hours.

3. Fluff the quinoa with a fork, garnish with the pumpkin seeds, and serve.

YIELD: **6 SERVINGS**

ACTIVE TIME: **20 MINUTES**

TOTAL TIME: **24 HOURS**

Rice Noodle Salad

This salad is perfect for those hot summer nights when you're terrified by the prospect of turning on the oven.

INGREDIENTS

FOR THE PEANUT SAUCE

JUICE OF 2 LIMES

2 TABLESPOONS MINCED GINGER

1 GARLIC CLOVE

¼ CUP BROWN SUGAR

2 TABLESPOONS FISH SAUCE

2 TABLESPOONS SOY SAUCE

½ CUP PEANUT BUTTER

FOR THE SALAD

1 LB. RICE STICK NOODLES

½ LB. CARROTS, PEELED AND SLICED THIN

1 RED BELL PEPPER, STEMMED, SEEDED, AND SLICED THIN

1 FRESNO PEPPER, STEMMED, SEEDED, AND SLICED THIN

2 JALAPEÑO PEPPERS, STEMMED, SEEDED, AND SLICED THIN

4 SCALLIONS, TRIMMED AND SLICED ON A BIAS

1 CUP FRESH BASIL LEAVES

¼ CUP CHOPPED FRESH CILANTRO

2 TABLESPOONS CHOPPED FRESH MINT

PEANUTS, CRUSHED, FOR GARNISH

DIRECTIONS

1. To prepare the peanut sauce, place all of the ingredients in a blender and puree until smooth. Transfer to the refrigerator and chill overnight.

2. To begin preparations for the salad, bring water to a boil in a large saucepan and add the noodles. Cook, while stirring, until the noodles are just tender, about 3 minutes. Drain and rinse with cold water.

3. Place the noodles and the remaining ingredients, except for the peanuts, in a salad bowl. Stir to combine, add the peanut sauce, and toss to coat. Garnish with the crushed peanuts and serve.

Raspberry & Tomato Gazpacho

YIELD: **4 SERVINGS**

ACTIVE TIME: **10 MINUTES**

TOTAL TIME: **4 HOURS**

Roasting the tomatoes brings out a sweetness that will be a tremendous boon when pitted against the slightly bitter aspect of the raspberries.

INGREDIENTS

2 TO 3 LARGE HEIRLOOM TOMATOES

1 CUP FRESH RASPBERRIES

2 GARLIC CLOVES

½ CUP PEELED AND SLICED CUCUMBER

2 TEASPOONS FRESH LEMON JUICE

2 TABLESPOONS OLIVE OIL

1 RED BELL PEPPER, STEMMED, SEEDED, AND CHOPPED

SALT AND PEPPER, TO TASTE

MINT LEAVES, FOR GARNISH

¼ CUP HEAVY CREAM, FOR GARNISH (OPTIONAL)

DIRECTIONS

1. Preheat the oven to 425°F. Place the tomatoes on a baking sheet and roast until they start to break down and darken, about 10 to 15 minutes. Remove from the oven and let cool slightly.

2. Place the tomatoes and the remaining ingredients, except for the garnishes, in a blender and puree until smooth. Transfer the mixture to the refrigerator for at least 3 hours, though refrigerating overnight recommended.

3. When ready to serve, ladle into bowls and garnish each serving with mint leaves and, if desired, approximately 1 tablespoon of heavy cream.

Spiced Buttermilk Stew with Spinach Dumplings

Like many Indian-inspired recipes, there are a lot of ingredients, but don't be daunted—the final result is well worth it.

INGREDIENTS

FOR THE STEW

8 CUPS BUTTERMILK

½ CUP CHICKPEA FLOUR

1 TABLESPOON TURMERIC

1 TEASPOON KOSHER SALT

1 TABLESPOON OLIVE OIL

1 TEASPOON CORIANDER SEEDS

1 TABLESPOON BLACK MUSTARD SEEDS

2 LARGE YELLOW ONIONS, SLICED INTO THIN HALF-MOONS

6 GARLIC CLOVES, MINCED

2 TABLESPOONS MINCED GINGER

1 TEASPOON AMCHOOR POWDER

2 SERRANO PEPPERS, STEMMED, SEEDED, AND MINCED

FOR THE DUMPLINGS

2 CUPS SPINACH, COOKED, DRAINED, AND CHOPPED

2 TEASPOONS KOSHER SALT

1 TEASPOON RED PEPPER FLAKES

1½ TEASPOONS CHAAT MASALA

1 CUP CHICKPEA FLOUR

DIRECTIONS

---

1. To begin preparations for the stew, place half of the buttermilk, the chickpea flour, turmeric, and salt in a blender and puree until smooth. Set the mixture aside.

2. Place the oil in a Dutch oven and warm over high heat. When the oil is shimmering, add the coriander and mustard seeds and cook, while stirring, until they start to pop.

3. Reduce the heat to medium and add the onions, garlic, ginger, amchoor powder, and serrano peppers. Sauté until the onions start to brown, about 5 minutes, and then pour in the buttermilk mixture. Add the remaining buttermilk, reduce the heat so that the stew gently simmers, and prepare the dumplings.

4. To prepare the dumplings, place the spinach, salt, red pepper flakes, and chaat masala in a mixing bowl and stir to combine. Add the chickpea flour and stir to incorporate. The dough should be quite stiff. Form tablespoons of the mixture into spheres.

5. Add the dumplings to the stew. When all of the dumplings have been added, cover the Dutch oven and cook for 10 minutes over low heat. Ladle into warmed bowls and serve.

NOTE: Amchoor is a sour powder made from the dried flesh of an unripe mango. Crucial to North Indian cuisine, you can find it at better grocery stores or online.

METRIC CONVERSIONS

U.S. Measurement	Approximate Metric Liquid Measurement	Approximate Metric Dry Measurement
1 teaspoon	5 ml	5 g
1 tablespoon or ½ ounce	15 ml	14 g
1 ounce or ⅛ cup	30 ml	29 g
¼ cup or 2 ounces	60 ml	57 g
⅓ cup	80 ml	76 g
½ cup or 4 ounces	120 ml	113 g
⅔ cup	160 ml	151 g
¾ cup or 6 ounces	180 ml	170 g
1 cup or 8 ounces or ½ pint	240 ml	227 g
1½ cups or 12 ounces	350 ml	340 g
2 cups or 1 pint or 16 ounces	475 ml	454 g
3 cups or 1½ pints	700 ml	680 g
4 cups or 2 pints or 1 quart	950 ml	908 g

INDEX

A

acorn squash, Jerk Acorn Squash with Baby Kale Salad & Maple Vinaigrette, 182–183

almonds, Garlic & Chili Broccolini, 204

andouille sausage, Jambalaya, 170–171

apples
Curried Chicken Salad with Apples & Pecans, 23
Peppered Pork Shoulder with Apples, Carrots & Onions, 99

Applewood-Smoked Ribs with Molasses BBQ Sauce, 96

arugula
Chilled Corn Salad, 212
Curried Chicken Salad with Apples & Pecans, 23
Grilled Chicken Paninis with Sun-Dried Tomato Aioli, 24

asparagus
Asparagus with Pancetta & Garlic Cream Sauce, 195
Spring Salad with Green Goddess Dressing, 216

avocados
Guacamole, 181
Tofu Tacos with Avocado Crema, 187

B

bacon, Grilled Chicken Paninis with Sun-Dried Tomato Aioli, 24

Barley, Sweet & Spicy Roasted, 188

basil
Marinated Short Ribs, 89
Rice Noodle Salad, 224
Scallops with Peaches & Basil-Cilantro Puree, 173
Swordfish with Citrus Salsa, 155
Thai Red Duck Curry, 51

BBQ Sauce
Applewood-Smoked Ribs with Molasses BBQ Sauce, 96
Coffee & Bourbon, 61

beans
Chili con Carne, 58
Green Bean & Tofu Casserole, 184

Puerto Rican Rice & Beans, 47

Shredded Chicken with Beans & Rice, 31

Veggie Burgers, 180

beef
Beef Shawarma, 82
Beef Stock, 67
Carne Asada, 69
Chili con Carne, 58
Chimichurri Strip Steak with Oregano Potatoes & Onions, 62–63
Crying Tiger Beef, 73
Curry Burgers, 132
Kefta with Chickpea Salad, 134–135
Kibbeh bil Sanieh, 81
Marinated Short Ribs, 89
Momos, 78
Papas Rellenas, 77
Pho, 66–67
Rib Eye with Salsa Verde & Porcini Mushroom Salt, 86
Sichuan Cumin Beef, 74
Steak au Poivre, 85
Steak with Peppers & Onions, 70
Sukiyaki, 65

Beef Stock
Braised Lamb with Minty Peas, 120
Mulligatawny, 136
Pho, 66–67
recipe for, 67

beets
Citrus & Sage Chicken with Golden Beets, 19
Coffee & Bourbon Brisket, 61
Jerk Chicken with Vegetables, 32–33

bird's eye chili peppers
Dudhi Kofta Curry, 192–193
Thai Mussels, 163
Thai Red Duck Curry, 51

black beans
Shredded Chicken with Beans & Rice, 31
Veggie Burgers, 180

blue cheese
for Blue Cheese Dressing, 49

Pork with Blue Cheese Polenta & Roasted Peach Hot Sauce, 104–105

Blue Cheese Dressing
Buffalo Wings, 48
recipe for, 49

bok choy
Grilled Lamb Loin with Quinoa & Radish Leaf Chimichurri, 122–123
Halibut with Braised Vegetables, 148
Pho, 66–67

Braised Lamb with Minty Peas, 120

Braised Pork Belly with Toasted Farro, Corn & Snap Peas, 102–103

Brisket, Coffee & Bourbon, 61

Broccolini, Garlic & Chili, 204

Brussels Sprouts with Hot Honey & Hazelnuts, Roasted, 203

Buffalo Wings, 48

Bulgogi with Musaengchae, 112

bulgur wheat
Chicken Thighs with Tabbouleh, 38–39
Kibbeh bil Sanieh, 81

burgers
Curry Burgers, 132
Veggie Burgers, 180

buttermilk
Blue Cheese Dressing, 49
Green Goddess Dressing, 216
Spiced Buttermilk Stew with Spinach Dumplings, 228

C

cabbage, Halibut with Braised Vegetables, 148

Cajun Tilapia, 151

cantaloupe, Melon, Cucumber & Prosciutto Salad with Mint Vinaigrette, 211

Carne Asada, 69

carrots
Braised Pork Belly with Toasted Farro, Corn & Snap Peas, 102–103
Chicken Stock, 30
Fish Stock, 149
Jerk Chicken with Vegetables, 32–33

Maple & Mustard Pork Tenderloin, 95

Marinated Short Ribs, 89

Peppered Pork Shoulder with Apples, Carrots & Onions, 99

Rice Noodle Salad, 224

Spicy Baby Carrots with Toasted Seed Granola, 196

Sweet & Spicy Roasted Barley, 188

cashews, Dudhi Kofta Curry, 192–193

cauliflower

    Chili-Dusted Cauliflower & Chickpea Salad, 214–215

    Roasted Cauliflower au Gratin, 207

cayenne peppers, Pork with Blue Cheese Polenta & Roasted Peach Hot Sauce, 104–105

celeriac, Smoked Trout with Celeriac Remoulade, 168

celery

    Beef Stock, 67

    Braised Pork Belly with Toasted Farro, Corn & Snap Peas, 102–103

    Chicken Stock, 30

    Curried Chicken Salad with Apples & Pecans, 23

    Fettuccine in Spicy Pork Sauce, 107

    Fish Stock, 149

    Jambalaya, 170–171

    Maple & Mustard Pork Tenderloin, 95

    Peppered Pork Shoulder with Apples, Carrots & Onions, 99

cheddar cheese, Grilled Chicken Paninis with Sun-Dried Tomato Aioli, 24

cheese. See individual cheeses

chicken

    Buffalo Wings, 48

    Chicken & Sausage Cacciatore with Rice, 12

    Chicken & Tomatillo Casserole, 40

    Chicken Fajitas, 44–45

    Chicken Kebabs, 43

    Chicken Stock, 30

    Chicken Thighs with Tabbouleh, 38–39

    Chicken Tsukune, 52

    Chicken Vindaloo, 27

    Chipotle Chicken Enchiladas, 16–17

    Cider-Glazed Cornish Hens, 35

    Citrus & Sage Chicken with Golden Beets, 19

    Coconut Curry Chicken with Basmati Rice, 20

    Curried Chicken Salad with Apples & Pecans, 23

    Grilled Chicken Paninis with Sun-Dried Tomato Aioli, 24

    Jambalaya, 170–171

    Jerk Chicken with Vegetables, 32–33

Korean Chicken Thighs with Sweet Potato Vermicelli, 36–37

Mojo Chicken, 28

Paella, 160

Puerto Rican Rice & Beans, 47

Sesame Chicken with Blistered Shishito Peppers, 15

Shredded Chicken with Beans & Rice, 31

Chicken Stock

    Braised Lamb with Minty Peas, 120

    Braised Pork Belly with Toasted Farro, Corn & Snap Peas, 102–103

    Chipotle Chicken Enchiladas, 16–17

    Fettuccine in Spicy Pork Sauce, 107

    Jambalaya, 170–171

    Kefta with Chickpea Salad, 134–135

    Maple & Mustard Pork Tenderloin, 95

    Paella, 160

    Peppered Pork Shoulder with Apples, Carrots & Onions, 99

    Pork with Blue Cheese Polenta & Roasted Peach Hot Sauce, 104–105

    Puerto Rican Rice & Beans, 47

    recipe for, 30

    Shredded Chicken with Beans & Rice, 31

    Takoyaki, 176

    Tare Sauce, 53

chickpeas

    Chili-Dusted Cauliflower & Chickpea Salad, 214–215

    Kefta with Chickpea Salad, 134–135

chiles de árbol, Shrimp Curry, 164

Chili con Carne, 58

chili peppers

    Hot Honey, 201

    Pho, 66–67

    Sichuan Cumin Beef, 74

Chili-Dusted Cauliflower & Chickpea Salad, 214–215

Chilled Corn Salad, 212

Chimichurri

    Chimichurri Strip Steak with Oregano Potatoes & Onions, 62–63

    Grilled Lamb Loin with Quinoa & Radish Leaf Chimichurri, 122–123

Chinese eggplants, Teriyaki Salmon & Vegetables, 143

chipotle peppers

    Chipotle Chicken Enchiladas, 16–17

    Grilled Corn with Chipotle Mayonnaise & Goat Cheese, 200

Chipotle Sausage & Peppers, 108

chorizo, Paella, 160

cider

    Applewood-Smoked Ribs with Molasses BBQ Sauce, 96

Cider-Glazed Cornish Hens, 35

cilantro

    Carne Asada, 69

    Chicken Fajitas, 44–45

    Chicken Thighs with Tabbouleh, 38–39

    Chili con Carne, 58

    Chilled Corn Salad, 212

    Chimichurri Strip Steak with Oregano Potatoes & Onions, 62–63

    Crying Tiger Beef, 73

    Curry Burgers, 132

    Halibut with Braised Vegetables, 148

    Kefta with Chickpea Salad, 134–135

    Lobster Tostadas with Corn Salsa & Cilantro-Lime Sour Cream, 174–175

    Mojo Chicken, 28

    Pho, 66–67

    Pico de Gallo, 45

    Punjabi Samosa, 190–191

    Red Snapper with Tomatillo Sauce, 152

    Rice Noodle Salad, 224

    Scallops with Peaches & Basil-Cilantro Puree, 173

    Shrimp Curry, 164

    Sichuan Cumin Beef, 74

    Spicy Lamb Chops with Raita, 116

    Swordfish with Citrus Salsa, 155

    Thai Mussels, 163

    Tofu Tacos with Avocado Crema, 187

Citrus & Sage Chicken with Golden Beets, 19

Citrus Salsa, Swordfish with, 155

coconut, Shrimp Curry, 164

coconut milk

    Coconut Curry Chicken with Basmati Rice, 20

    Halibut with Braised Vegetables, 148

    Mulligatawny, 136

    Shrimp Curry, 164

    Thai Mussels, 163

    Thai Red Duck Curry, 51

Coffee & Bourbon BBQ Sauce, 61

Coffee & Bourbon Brisket, 61

corn

    Braised Pork Belly with Toasted Farro, Corn & Snap Peas, 102–103

    Chilled Corn Salad, 212

    Grilled Corn with Chipotle Mayonnaise & Goat Cheese, 200

    Lamb Kebabs with Succotash, 119

    Lobster Tostadas with Corn Salsa & Cilantro-Lime Sour Cream, 174–175

    Tofu Tacos with Avocado Crema, 187

    Veggie Burgers, 180

Corn Tortillas
    Carne Asada, 69
    Chicken & Tomatillo Casserole, 40
    Chicken Fajitas, 44–45
    Chipotle Chicken Enchiladas, 16–17
    Lobster Tostadas with Corn Salsa & Cilantro-Lime Sour Cream, 174–175
    recipe for, 68
    Red Snapper with Tomatillo Sauce, 152
    Tofu Tacos with Avocado Crema, 187
Cornish Hens, Cider-Glazed, 35
cotija cheese
    Chicken & Tomatillo Casserole, 40
    Chilled Corn Salad, 212
    Chipotle Chicken Enchiladas, 16–17
cranberries
    Jerk Acorn Squash with Baby Kale Salad & Maple Vinaigrette, 182–183
    Toasted Seed Granola, 197
Crying Tiger Beef, 73
cucumbers
    Beef Shawarma, 82
    Melon, Cucumber & Prosciutto Salad with Mint Vinaigrette, 211
    Raspberry & Tomato Gazpacho, 227
    Spicy Lamb Chops with Raita, 116
    Spicy Pickles, 208
    Summer Salad with Oregano Vinaigrette, 219
    Swordfish with Citrus Salsa, 155
Cumin Beef, Sichuan, 74
Curried Chicken Salad with Apples & Pecans, 23
Curry Burgers, 132
Curry Chicken with Basmati Rice, Coconut, 20

D

daikon radish, Musaengchae, 113
Dashi Broth, 64
    Sukiyaki, 65
Dry Rub
    Coffee & Bourbon Brisket, 61
    recipe for, 60
duck, Thai Red Duck Curry, 51
duck fat, 50
Dudhi Kofta Curry, 192–193
Dukkah
    Dukkah-Spiced Sea Bass, 147
    recipe for, 146
Dumplings, Spiced Buttermilk Stew with Spinach, 228

E

edamame, Lamb Kebabs with Succotash, 119

eggplants
    Halibut with Braised Vegetables, 148
    Teriyaki Salmon & Vegetables, 143
emmental cheese, Roasted Cauliflower au Gratin, 207
Enchiladas, Chipotle Chicken, 16–17

F

Fajitas, Chicken, 44–45
Farro, Corn & Snap Peas, Braised Pork Belly with Toasted, 102–103
feta cheese
    Chilled Corn Salad, 212
    Jerk Acorn Squash with Baby Kale Salad & Maple Vinaigrette, 182–183
    Melon, Cucumber & Prosciutto Salad with Mint Vinaigrette, 211
Fettuccine in Spicy Pork Sauce, 107
fire-roasted tomatoes, Chipotle Sausage & Peppers, 108
fish. See seafood; individual fish
Fish Stock
    Halibut with Braised Vegetables, 148
    recipe for, 149
Five-Spice Turkey Breast, 55
fresno peppers
    Chili-Dusted Cauliflower & Chickpea Salad, 214–215
    Rice Noodle Salad, 224

G

garbanzo beans, Kefta with Chickpea Salad, 134–135
garlic
    Garlic & Chili Broccolini, 204
    Garlic & Herb Crust, Roasted Rack of Lamb with, 124
    Garlic Cream Sauce, Asparagus with Pancetta &, 195
    Garlic Shrimp, 167
Gazpacho, Raspberry & Tomato, 227
Gingery Red Pepper Sauce, 79
Goat Cheese, Grilled Corn with Chipotle Mayonnaise &, 200
Golden Beets, Citrus & Sage Chicken with, 19
Greek yogurt. See yogurt
Green Bean & Tofu Casserole, 184
Green Goddess Dressing, Spring Salad with, 216
Grilled Chicken Paninis with Sun-Dried Tomato Aioli, 24
Grilled Corn with Chipotle Mayonnaise & Goat Cheese, 200
Grilled Lamb Loin with Quinoa & Radish Leaf Chimichurri, 122–123
Grilled Tuna Steaks with Wasabi Butter, 156

Guacamole
    recipe for, 181
    Red Snapper with Tomatillo Sauce, 152
    Veggie Burgers, 180

H

habanero peppers
    Chipotle Sausage & Peppers, 108
    Halibut with Braised Vegetables, 148
    Jerk Chicken with Vegetables, 32–33
    Spicy Pickles, 208
Halibut with Braised Vegetables, 148
Hash, Lamb & Sweet Potato, 127
hazelnuts
    Dukkah, 146
    Roasted Brussels Sprouts with Hot Honey & Hazelnuts, 203
Herring, Pickled Fried, 144
honey
    Applewood-Smoked Ribs with Molasses BBQ Sauce, 96
    Braised Lamb with Minty Peas, 120
    Cider-Glazed Cornish Hens, 35
    Green Bean & Tofu Casserole, 184
    Hot Honey, 201
    Melon, Cucumber & Prosciutto Salad with Mint Vinaigrette, 211
    Roasted Brussels Sprouts with Hot Honey & Hazelnuts, 203
    Shaved Squash Salad with Herb Vinaigrette, 220
    Summer Salad with Oregano Vinaigrette, 219
    Toasted Seed Granola, 197
honeydew melon, Melon, Cucumber & Prosciutto Salad with Mint Vinaigrette, 211
Hot Honey
    recipe for, 201
    Roasted Brussels Sprouts with Hot Honey & Hazelnuts, 203

J

jalapeño peppers
    Carne Asada, 69
    Chicken Fajitas, 44–45
    Chili con Carne, 58
    Chimichurri Strip Steak with Oregano Potatoes & Onions, 62–63
    Lobster Tostadas with Corn Salsa & Cilantro-Lime Sour Cream, 174–175
    Melon, Cucumber & Prosciutto Salad with Mint Vinaigrette, 211
    Pico de Gallo, 45
    Pork with Blue Cheese Polenta & Roasted Peach Hot Sauce, 104–105

Punjabi Samosa, 190–191

Rice Noodle Salad, 224

Scallops with Peaches & Basil-Cilantro Puree, 173

Shredded Chicken with Beans & Rice, 31

Tofu Tacos with Avocado Crema, 187

Jambalaya, 170–171

Jerk Acorn Squash with Baby Kale Salad & Maple Vinaigrette, 182–183

Jerk Chicken with Vegetables, 32–33

Jerk Marinade

Jerk Acorn Squash with Baby Kale Salad & Maple Vinaigrette, 182–183

recipe for, 183

K

kale

Halibut with Braised Vegetables, 148

Jerk Acorn Squash with Baby Kale Salad & Maple Vinaigrette, 182–183

Kefta with Chickpea Salad, 134–135

Kibbeh bil Sanieh, 81

kidney beans, Puerto Rican Rice & Beans, 47

kielbasa, Chipotle Sausage & Peppers, 108

Kofta Curry, Dudhi, 192–193

Korean Chicken Thighs with Sweet Potato Vermicelli, 36–37

L

lamb

Braised Lamb with Minty Peas, 120

Curry Burgers, 132

Grilled Lamb Loin with Quinoa & Radish Leaf Chimichurri, 122–123

Kefta with Chickpea Salad, 134–135

Lamb & Sweet Potato Hash, 127

Lamb Kebabs with Succotash, 119

Leg of Lamb with Rosemary & Mustard Marinade, 128

Mulligatawny, 136

Roasted Rack of Lamb with Garlic & Herb Crust, 124

Rogan Josh, 131

Spicy Lamb Chops with Raita, 116

Lamb Marinade

Grilled Lamb Loin with Quinoa & Radish Leaf Chimichurri, 122–123

recipe for, 123

leeks

Citrus & Sage Chicken with Golden Beets, 19

Fish Stock, 149

Leg of Lamb with Rosemary & Mustard Marinade, 128

lettuce

Spring Salad with Green Goddess Dressing, 216

Summer Salad with Oregano Vinaigrette, 219

Lobster Tostadas with Corn Salsa & Cilantro-Lime Sour Cream, 174–175

M

Mahi-Mahi, Spicy, 159

mango, Swordfish with Citrus Salsa, 155

Maple & Mustard Pork Tenderloin, 95

Maple Vinaigrette, Jerk Acorn Squash with Baby Kale Salad &, 182–183

Marinated Short Ribs, 89

Melon, Cucumber & Prosciutto Salad with Mint Vinaigrette, 211

metric conversions, 232

mint

Braised Lamb with Minty Peas, 120

Melon, Cucumber & Prosciutto Salad with Mint Vinaigrette, 211

Mint Vinaigrette, 211

Mojo Chicken, 28

Molasses BBQ Sauce, Applewood-Smoked Ribs with, 96

Momos, 78

Mulligatawny, 136

Musaengchae

Bulgogi with Musaengchae, 112

recipe for, 113

mushrooms

Green Bean & Tofu Casserole, 184

Korean Chicken Thighs with Sweet Potato Vermicelli, 36–37

Lamb Kebabs with Succotash, 119

Rib Eye with Salsa Verde & Porcini Mushroom Salt, 86

Sukiyaki, 65

mussels

Paella, 160

Thai Mussels, 163

Mustard Marinade, Leg of Lamb with Rosemary &, 128

Mustard Pork Tenderloin, Maple &, 95

N

napa cabbage

Korean Chicken Thighs with Sweet Potato Vermicelli, 36–37

Sukiyaki, 65

nectarines, Coffee & Bourbon Brisket, 61

O

octopus, Takoyaki, 176

onions

Beef Shawarma, 82

Braised Lamb with Minty Peas, 120

Braised Pork Belly with Toasted Farro, Corn & Snap Peas, 102–103

Chimichurri Strip Steak with Oregano Potatoes & Onions, 62–63

Dudhi Kofta Curry, 192–193

Fettuccine in Spicy Pork Sauce, 107

Fish Stock, 149

Guacamole, 181

Jambalaya, 170–171

Kibbeh bil Sanieh, 81

Lamb & Sweet Potato Hash, 127

Lamb Kebabs with Succotash, 119

Maple & Mustard Pork Tenderloin, 95

Marinated Short Ribs, 89

Momos, 78

Paella, 160

Papas Rellenas, 77

Peppered Pork Shoulder with Apples, Carrots & Onions, 99

Pickled Fried Herring, 144

Pork with Blue Cheese Polenta & Roasted Peach Hot Sauce, 104–105

Rogan Josh, 131

Sichuan Cumin Beef, 74

Sofrito & Quinoa Salad, 223

Spiced Buttermilk Stew with Spinach Dumplings, 228

Spicy Pickles, 208

Steak with Peppers & Onions, 70

Sweet & Spicy Roasted Barley, 188

Tofu Tacos with Avocado Crema, 187

Oregano Vinaigrette, Summer Salad with, 219

P

Paella, 160

pancetta

Asparagus with Pancetta & Garlic Cream Sauce, 195

Paella, 160

Paninis with Sun-Dried Tomato Aioli, Grilled Chicken, 24

Papas Rellenas, 77

parmesan cheese

Roasted Brussels Sprouts with Hot Honey & Hazelnuts, 203

Roasted Cauliflower au Gratin, 207

Summer Salad with Oregano Vinaigrette, 219

Zucchini Fritters with Sumac Yogurt, 199

parsley

Kefta with Chickpea Salad, 134–135

Rib Eye with Salsa Verde & Porcini Mushroom Salt, 86

Spring Salad with Green Goddess Dressing, 216

pasilla peppers, Sweet & Spicy Roasted Barley, 188

pasta, Fettuccine in Spicy Pork Sauce, 107

peaches
Coffee & Bourbon Brisket, 61
Pork with Blue Cheese Polenta & Roasted Peach Hot Sauce, 104–105
Scallops with Peaches & Basil-Cilantro Puree, 173

Peanut Sauce, Rice Noodle Salad, 224

peanuts
Dukkah, 146
Rice Noodle Salad, 224

peas
Braised Lamb with Minty Peas, 120
Braised Pork Belly with Toasted Farro, Corn & Snap Peas, 102–103
Paella, 160
Spring Salad with Green Goddess Dressing, 216

Pecans, Curried Chicken Salad with Apples &, 23

Peppered Pork Shoulder with Apples, Carrots & Onions, 99

peppers, hot
Carne Asada, 69
Chicken & Tomatillo Casserole, 40
Chicken Fajitas, 44–45
Chili con Carne, 58
Chili-Dusted Cauliflower & Chickpea Salad, 214–215
Chilled Corn Salad, 212
Chimichurri Strip Steak with Oregano Potatoes & Onions, 62–63
Chipotle Chicken Enchiladas, 16–17
Chipotle Sausage & Peppers, 108
Dudhi Kofta Curry, 192–193
Grilled Corn with Chipotle Mayonnaise & Goat Cheese, 200
Halibut with Braised Vegetables, 148
Hot Honey, 201
Jerk Chicken with Vegetables, 32–33
Lamb & Sweet Potato Hash, 127
Lobster Tostadas with Corn Salsa & Cilantro-Lime Sour Cream, 174–175
Melon, Cucumber & Prosciutto Salad with Mint Vinaigrette, 211
Pho, 66–67
Pico de Gallo, 45
Pork with Blue Cheese Polenta & Roasted Peach Hot Sauce, 104–105
Punjabi Samosa, 190–191
Red Snapper with Tomatillo Sauce, 152
Rice Noodle Salad, 224

Scallops with Peaches & Basil-Cilantro Puree, 173
Sesame Chicken with Blistered, 15
Shredded Chicken with Beans & Rice, 31
Shrimp Curry, 164
Sichuan Cumin Beef, 74
Sofrito, 46
Sofrito & Quinoa Salad, 223
Spiced Buttermilk Stew with Spinach Dumplings, 228
Spicy Pickles, 208
Sweet & Spicy Roasted Barley, 188
Thai Mussels, 163
Thai Red Duck Curry, 51
Tofu Tacos with Avocado Crema, 187

peppers, sweet
Chicken Fajitas, 44–45
Chili con Carne, 58
Chipotle Sausage & Peppers, 108
Coconut Curry Chicken with Basmati Rice, 20
Gingery Red Pepper Sauce, 79
Halibut with Braised Vegetables, 148
Jambalaya, 170–171
Lamb Kebabs with Succotash, 119
Mojo Chicken, 28
Paella, 160
Papas Rellenas, 77
Raspberry & Tomato Gazpacho, 227
Rice Noodle Salad, 224
Sesame Chicken with Blistered Shishito Peppers, 15
Shaved Squash Salad with Herb Vinaigrette, 220
Sofrito, 46
Sofrito & Quinoa Salad, 223
Spicy Pickles, 208
Steak with Peppers & Onions, 70
Swordfish with Citrus Salsa, 155
Teriyaki Salmon & Vegetables, 143
Veggie Burgers, 180

Pho, 66–67

Pickled Fried Herring, 144

Pico de Gallo, Chicken Fajitas, 44–45

pine needles, Pickled Fried Herring, 144

pine nuts, Kibbeh bil Sanieh, 81

pineapple
Swordfish with Citrus Salsa, 155
Thai Red Duck Curry, 51

pistachios, Dukkah, 146

poblano peppers
Chicken & Tomatillo Casserole, 40
Chilled Corn Salad, 212
Lamb & Sweet Potato Hash, 127
Sofrito, 46

Sofrito & Quinoa Salad, 223

Porchetta, 111

Porcini Mushroom Salt, Rib Eye with Salsa Verde &, 86

pork
Braised Pork Belly with Toasted Farro, Corn & Snap Peas, 102–103
Bulgogi with Musaengchae, 112
Fettuccine in Spicy Pork Sauce, 107
Maple & Mustard Pork Tenderloin, 95
Peppered Pork Shoulder with Apples, Carrots & Onions, 99
Porchetta, 111
Pork with Blue Cheese Polenta & Roasted Peach Hot Sauce, 104–105
Shengjian Baozi, 100–101
Spicy Tonkatsu, 92
See also bacon; pancetta; sausage

potatoes
Applewood-Smoked Ribs with Molasses BBQ Sauce, 96
Chimichurri Strip Steak with Oregano Potatoes & Onions, 62–63
Chipotle Chicken Enchiladas, 16–17
Maple & Mustard Pork Tenderloin, 95
Papas Rellenas, 77
Pickled Fried Herring, 144
Punjabi Samosa, 190–191

Prosciutto Salad with Mint Vinaigrette, Melon, Cucumber &, 211

Puerto Rican Rice & Beans, 47

pumpkin seeds
Dukkah, 146
Sofrito & Quinoa Salad, 223

Punjabi Samosa, 190–191

Q

quinoa
Grilled Lamb Loin with Quinoa & Radish Leaf Chimichurri, 122–123
Sofrito & Quinoa Salad, 223

R

radishes
Grilled Lamb Loin with Quinoa & Radish Leaf Chimichurri, 122–123
Spring Salad with Green Goddess Dressing, 216

raisins
Dudhi Kofta Curry, 192–193
Papas Rellenas, 77

Raita, Spicy Lamb Chops with, 116

Raspberry & Tomato Gazpacho, 227

Red Pepper Sauce, Gingery, 79

Red Snapper with Tomatillo Sauce, 152

rice
- Chicken & Sausage Cacciatore with Rice, 12
- Coconut Curry Chicken with Basmati Rice, 20
- Jambalaya, 170–171
- Mulligatawny, 136
- Paella, 160
- Puerto Rican Rice & Beans, 47
- Shredded Chicken with Beans & Rice, 31
- Tea-Smoked Salmon, 140
- Thai Mussels, 163
- Thai Red Duck Curry, 51
- Toasted Rice Powder, 72

rice noodles
- Pho, 66–67
- Rice Noodle Salad, 224
- Thai Mussels, 163

Roasted Brussels Sprouts with Hot Honey & Hazelnuts, 203

Roasted Cauliflower au Gratin, 207

Roasted Rack of Lamb with Garlic & Herb Crust, 124

Rogan Josh, 131

Rosemary & Mustard Marinade, Leg of Lamb with, 128

S

Sage Chicken with Golden Beets, Citrus &, 19

salads
- Chili-Dusted Cauliflower & Chickpea Salad, 214–215
- Chilled Corn Salad, 212
- Curried Chicken Salad with Apples & Pecans, 23
- Jerk Acorn Squash with Baby Kale Salad & Maple Vinaigrette, 182–183
- Kefta with Chickpea Salad, 134–135
- Melon, Cucumber & Prosciutto Salad with Mint Vinaigrette, 211
- Rice Noodle Salad, 224
- Shaved Squash Salad with Herb Vinaigrette, 220
- Smoked Trout with Celeriac Remoulade, 168
- Sofrito & Quinoa Salad, 223
- Spring Salad with Green Goddess Dressing, 216
- Summer Salad with Oregano Vinaigrette, 219

salmon
- Tea-Smoked Salmon, 140
- Teriyaki Salmon & Vegetables, 143

Salsa Verde (parsley-based), 86

Salsa Verde (tomatillo-based), 40

Samosa, Punjabi, 190–191

sausage
- Chicken & Sausage Cacciatore with Rice, 12
- Chipotle Sausage & Peppers, 108
- Jambalaya, 170–171
- Scallops with Peaches & Basil-Cilantro Puree, 173

Sea Bass, Dukkah-Spiced, 147

seafood
- Cajun Tilapia, 151
- Dukkah-Spiced Sea Bass, 147
- Fish Stock, 149
- Garlic Shrimp, 167
- Grilled Tuna Steaks with Wasabi Butter, 156
- Halibut with Braised Vegetables, 148
- Lobster Tostadas with Corn Salsa & Cilantro-Lime Sour Cream, 174–175
- Paella, 160
- Pickled Fried Herring, 144
- Red Snapper with Tomatillo Sauce, 152
- Scallops with Peaches & Basil-Cilantro Puree, 173
- Shrimp Curry, 164
- Smoked Trout with Celeriac Remoulade, 168
- Spicy Mahi-Mahi, 159
- Swordfish with Citrus Salsa, 155
- Takoyaki, 176
- Tea-Smoked Salmon, 140
- Teriyaki Salmon & Vegetables, 143
- Thai Mussels, 163

serrano peppers
- Red Snapper with Tomatillo Sauce, 152
- Shrimp Curry, 164
- Spiced Buttermilk Stew with Spinach Dumplings, 228

Sesame Chicken with Blistered Shishito Peppers, 15

Shaved Squash Salad with Herb Vinaigrette, 220

Shengjian Baozi, 100–101

Shishito Peppers, Sesame Chicken with Blistered, 15

Shredded Chicken with Beans & Rice, 31

shrimp
- Garlic Shrimp, 167
- Jambalaya, 170–171
- Paella, 160
- Shrimp Curry, 164

Sichuan Cumin Beef, 74

Smoked Trout with Celeriac Remoulade, 168

Sofrito
- Puerto Rican Rice & Beans, 47
- recipe for, 46

Sofrito & Quinoa Salad, 223

Sour Cream, Cilantro-Lime, 174–175

spatchcocking, 34

Spiced Buttermilk Stew with Spinach Dumplings, 228

Spicy Baby Carrots with Toasted Seed Granola, 196

Spicy Lamb Chops with Raita, 116

Spicy Mahi-Mahi, 159

Spicy Pickles, 208

Spicy Tonkatsu, 92

spinach
- Dukkah-Spiced Sea Bass, 147
- Spiced Buttermilk Stew with Spinach Dumplings, 228
- Sukiyaki, 65

Spring Salad with Green Goddess Dressing, 216

squash
- Jerk Acorn Squash with Baby Kale Salad & Maple Vinaigrette, 182–183
- Shaved Squash Salad with Herb Vinaigrette, 220
- Toasted Seed Granola, 197
- See also zucchini

Steak au Poivre, 85

Steak with Peppers & Onions, 70

Strip Steak with Oregano Potatoes & Onions, Chimichurri, 62–63

Succotash, Lamb Kebabs with, 119

Sukiyaki, 65

Sumac Yogurt, Zucchini Fritters with, 199

Summer Salad with Oregano Vinaigrette, 219

Sun-Dried Tomato Aioli, Grilled Chicken Paninis with, 24

Sweet & Spicy Roasted Barley, 188

sweet potatoes
- Chimichurri Strip Steak with Oregano Potatoes & Onions, 62–63
- Halibut with Braised Vegetables, 148
- Jerk Chicken with Vegetables, 32–33
- Korean Chicken Thighs with Sweet Potato Vermicelli, 36–37
- Lamb & Sweet Potato Hash, 127

Swordfish with Citrus Salsa, 155

T

Tabbouleh, Chicken Thighs with, 38–39

Tacos with Avocado Crema, Tofu, 187

Takoyaki, 176

Takoyaki Sauce
- recipe for, 177
- Takoyaki, 176

Tare Sauce
- Chicken Tsukune, 52

recipe for, 53
Tea-Smoked Salmon, 140
Teriyaki Salmon & Vegetables, 143
Teriyaki Sauce, 143
Thai Mussels, 163
Thai Red Duck Curry, 51
Tilapia, Cajun, 151
time, necessity of, 7
Toasted Rice Powder
    Crying Tiger Beef, 73
    recipe for, 72
Toasted Seed Granola
    recipe for, 197
    Spicy Baby Carrots with Toasted
      Seed Granola, 196
tofu
    Green Bean & Tofu Casserole, 184
    Sukiyaki, 65
    Tofu Tacos with Avocado Crema, 187
tomatillos
    Chicken & Tomatillo Casserole, 40
    Red Snapper with Tomatillo Sauce,
      152
Tomato Chutney
    Curry Burgers, 132
    recipe for, 133
tomatoes
    Beef Shawarma, 82
    Chicken & Sausage Cacciatore with
      Rice, 12
    Chicken & Tomatillo Casserole, 40
    Chicken Thighs with Tabbouleh,
      38–39
    Chicken Vindaloo, 27
    Chili con Carne, 58
    Chipotle Chicken Enchiladas, 16–17
    Chipotle Sausage & Peppers, 108
    Dudhi Kofta Curry, 192–193
    Grilled Chicken Paninis with Sun-
      Dried Tomato Aioli, 24
    Guacamole, 181
    Jambalaya, 170–171
    Paella, 160
    Pico de Gallo, 45
    Raspberry & Tomato Gazpacho, 227
    Rogan Josh, 131
    Shaved Squash Salad with Herb
      Vinaigrette, 220
    Shredded Chicken with Beans &
      Rice, 31
    Shrimp Curry, 164
    Sofrito, 46
    Sofrito & Quinoa Salad, 223
    Summer Salad with Oregano
      Vinaigrette, 219
    Thai Red Duck Curry, 51
    Tofu Tacos with Avocado Crema, 187

Tomato Chutney, 133
Tuna Steaks with Wasabi Butter, Grilled,
    156
Turkey Breast, Five-Spice, 55
turnips, Jerk Chicken with Vegetables,
    32–33

U
udon noodles, Sukiyaki, 65

V
Vegetable Stock, Peppered Pork
    Shoulder with Apples, Carrots &
    Onions, 99
vegetables. See individual vegetables
Veggie Burgers, 180
Vermicelli, Korean Chicken Thighs with
    Sweet Potato, 36–37

W
Wasabi Butter, Grilled Tuna Steaks with,
    156
whitefish, Fish Stock, 149

Y
yogurt
    Beef Shawarma, 82
    Chicken Kebabs, 43
    Dukkah-Spiced Sea Bass, 147
    Rogan Josh, 131
    Spicy Lamb Chops with Raita, 116
    Zucchini Fritters with Sumac Yogurt,
      199

Z
zucchini
    Dudhi Kofta Curry, 192–193
    Shaved Squash Salad with Herb
      Vinaigrette, 220
    Zucchini Fritters with Sumac Yogurt,
      199

ABOUT CIDER MILL PRESS
BOOK PUBLISHERS

❊ ❊ ❊

Good ideas ripen with time. From seed to harvest,
Cider Mill Press brings fine reading, information,
and entertainment together between the covers of its
creatively crafted books. Our Cider Mill bears fruit twice
a year, publishing a new crop of titles each spring and fall.

CIDER MILL PRESS

BOOK PUBLISHERS
KENNEBUNKPORT, MAINE

"Where Good Books Are Ready for Press"

Visit us online at
www.cidermillpress.com
or write to us at
PO Box 454
12 Spring St.
Kennebunkport, Maine 04046